BIG
FORCE
NEGOTIATION

THE EIGHT *SKILLS* YOU *NEED* TO NEGOTIATE WITH POWER

BIG FORCE
NEGOTIATION

THE EIGHT *SKILLS* YOU *NEED* TO NEGOTIATE WITH POWER

TERRANCE W. MOORE

Two Harbors Press
212 3rd Avenue North, Suite 290
Minneapolis, MN 55401
612.455.2293
www.TwoHarborsPress.com

ISBN-13: 978-1-937293-44-4
LCCN: 2011945998

Distributed by Itasca Books

Cover Design and Typeset by James Arneson

Printed in the United States of America

TABLE OF CONTENTS

INTRODUCTION
It's Better to be Better

It's the 2009 Major League Baseball playoffs. My favorite team, the Minnesota Twins, is facing the New York Yankees in a divisional playoff series. The Yankees have better players than the Twins. The Yankees won all seven regular season games between the two teams. The Yankees play in the strongest division in baseball, and score more runs than any other major-league team—they won more games (103) than any team in baseball. During the season, they scored ninety-eight more runs and allowed twelve fewer runs than the Twins. Their payroll of $201 million is three times higher than the Twins payroll of $65 million. The Yankees starting pitcher in game one of the playoff series is C.C. Sabathia, who has one hundred and thirty-six wins in nine major-league seasons. The Twins start rookie Brian Duensing, who has only five career wins.

Meanwhile, the Twins play in the weakest division in baseball. They won the AL Central Division by the narrowest margin. Trailing by seven games in September, they managed to catch the Detroit Tigers and create a tie after completion of the 162-game season. This forced a rare additional game, which the Twins finally won in the twelfth inning. So the Twins became champions of the weakest division in baseball by just a whisker.

On this particular game day, it's clear the Yankees are a stronger team than the Twins. Everyone expects the Yankees to win. Yet the Twins, coming off an emotional twelve-inning win the night before, have heart. And the Twins have some true stars on the team. . . . Well, the scrappy Twins manage to take a 2–0 lead in the top of the third inning. Things look possible for my Minnesota boys.

But it all changes in the bottom of the third inning. All-star Derek Jeter ties the game with a two-run home run. In the fourth inning, the Yankees score to take the lead. In the fifth inning they add three more runs and then tally another in the seventh inning. Final score: Yankees 7, Twins 2.

Why did the Yankees beat the Twins? Their team as a whole was just better than the Twins. It's that simple. The Twins can do everything right, but the Yankees will still win more games because the Yankees are just better. The better team wins more games in the long run. This is why we bet on the fastest horses.

The same principle applies to negotiation. You can prepare well, you can develop strategy, and you can understand exactly what will get the best deal for your side, but if you can't execute your game plan you will not succeed in the long run. You must be able to hit the curve ball to play in the major leagues.

This means you have to do the right things along the way to make yourself a better negotiator. This book is not about how you prepare for a particular negotiation session but rather how you prepare yourself to be better at every session you engage in.

A BIG FORCE negotiator needs to master eight fundamental skills of negotiation. I call these the "BIG FORCE skills" because it helps me remember them—and it's a cool name. The skills you need to have (or have on your team) are:

1. Body Language and Nonverbal Communication
2. Interviewing and Listening
3. Getting Ready: Preparation
4. Financial Analysis
5. Opposition and Industry Knowledge
6. Research
7. Communication Skills
8. Endgame and Closing

These skills take years to master. Many of these skills are also college majors—for example, you can earn degrees in finance or communications—and professionals spend years perfecting the art of interrogation (which also incorporates many of the skills above). As you might expect, it will take years of work to become a BIG FORCE negotiator.

The goal of this book is not to complete your journey as a master negotiator but rather to begin it. If you can come away with an understanding of your own strengths and weaknesses with respect to the eight fundamental skills and know how to improve them, you will be a better negotiator.

The secondary benefit of this book is that it helps you build a negotiation team. If, for example, you are not adept at financial analysis, then you need someone on your team who is an expert. In an ideal world, your team members' expertise will encompass all eight skills. You must put together a team that covers as many of these skills as possible for any important negotiation.

Once you understand the eight skills required to master negotiation, you will be able to recognize your opponent's weakness. By understanding your opponent, you will be able to exploit their weakness and avoid battling them where they are strong.

The best negotiators are experts in most of these skill areas and strong in the others. On big deals, negotiating teams should include expertise in all of these areas. Most people try to get by on less than half of these skills. Remember, you may not be able to obtain expertise in all eight areas, but you can get better at all of them. The better you are, the better your results will be.

"It's just business." This phrase allows successful and unsuccessful negotiators alike to pretend that a business deal has no personal impact. Treating negotiations as "just business" lowers the stakes and minimizes stress by denying that the results really have an impact on the negotiator personally.

And negotiators need this buffer because even the coldest business negotiation is ultimately personal. Negotiation will be more or less personal depending on the nature of the transaction. Fighting over lease rates is less personal than fighting over custody of your children, but winning the lease rates battle is still personal to the negotiator. The personal nature of negotiations is what drives us toward "winning" the transaction.

This book is based on the principle that negotiating results flow directly from the people involved in the negotiation. I hope to improve your results by helping you understand how to obtain the skills that will make you a better negotiator.

A negotiation is successful when, from your vantage point, the result is acceptable to you. An unsuccessful negotiation is one in which either no agreement is reached (assuming you wanted to reach one) or you agree to things you don't want to agree to. If you study the steps in this book, you will become a better negotiator. You will increase your chances for successful negotiations.

To achieve a successful negotiation, the other side must be motivated to make an agreement with you. To maximize your ability to motivate your counterparts, you must first understand how motivation works. Abraham Maslow (1908–70) wrote what is still considered the definitive work on motivation, *Motivation and Personality* (1954). Maslow characterized human motivation on five levels, ranging from a basic physical need to a desire for self-actualization.

With Maslow's theory in mind, negotiation preparation can be divided into two categories. You must first prepare yourself by obtaining the skills necessary to make you a BIG FORCE Negotiator. You must also prepare strategically and tactically for each particular negotiation project, because each project is unique. Both of these areas are absolutely critical to successful outcomes.

This book is designed to help improve your results in the negotiations you conduct every day. If you understand motivation and master all of the above skills, you will get through many day-to-day negotiations without significant preparation. If you master the skills of preparation as well, then you will maximize your chance for successful negotiation on any deal of any size, anywhere in the world.

If you are an expert in all of these skills, you are a true star, a BIG FORCE.

THE 8 SKILLS OF

BIG FORCE NEGOTIATION

SKILL #1
Body Language and Nonverbal Communication

Body language and nonverbal communication involve the art and science of hearing what is not said. The ability to read nonverbal signals is often the difference between a failed negotiation and a successful one. Ironically, this complicated skill has one of the shortest chapters in this book. This is because this skill requires more outside reading and practice than any other. Nonverbal communication takes years of practice to master. On the other hand, learning the basics can give you a big advantage right away.

Study Up and Practice

Years ago, I decided to read everything I could find on nonverbal communication. I recommend this process. Start with *How to Read a Person Like a Book* by Gerard Nierenberg (1971). Then read a few more books on the subject. Finally, go back to Nierenberg and read his book again. (Nierenberg is a giant in the negotiation world.)

The key to nonverbal communication is practice. Watch people interacting around you. Nierenberg talks about studying people at the airport. You can do it anywhere. Try to figure out whether the woman in line is interested in the man talking to her. Does the bartender enjoy his job? Does the lector at church really want to go up there and do the reading? Follow the keys in these books and you will pick up the habit of observation fairly quickly.

Observation

The skill of observation will help you deal with people who are trying to fool you. As a young lawyer, I sometimes encountered colleagues who tried to gain an edge by being aggressive. They would yell. They would put their finger in my chest. A senior lawyer taught me how to effectively defuse these attacks. First, if you think a person is just acting angry, then you can smile or scoff at their behavior, letting them know you recognize it as posturing. This will gain respect, at least to the point of stopping the fake blustering. However, if you scoff or laugh at someone who is truly angry, it will incite the situation. And if you are insecure about the person's true mood, laughing can appear to be a nervous reaction, causing the bully to attack with vigor. So it is critical to be confident in your reading of your opponent's true purpose.

Here is what my mentor taught me. As your counterparts are blustering, carefully observe three things: where they are looking, the color of their cheeks, and the position of their hands.

First, look at the eyes. Is the person looking at you directly or looking towards you and then away? The more a person looks anywhere except at your face, the more likely it is that he or she is posturing. Next, look at his cheeks. Are they redder than normal? Anger increases blood pressure, and this will be apparent on the person's face. But be warned: an absence of red means a person is probably faking it; yet the presence of red does not guarantee true anger. This symptom is easy to fake, especially if someone uses the trick often. Lastly, observe the person's hands. Someone who is truly angry will show stress in the hands. The fingers might be fully extended or in a fist, but they will show tension. If not, then the person is probably posturing. Further, if someone points in your general direction, but not directly at you, he or she is probably faking anger. You can observe these three things and roll them all together to reach your conclusion. Then decide how to respond.

Involuntary Signals

Nonverbal communication signals are often given involuntarily. People who talk through their hand don't believe what they are saying. They are probably lying, or at least speaking less than the whole truth. People who cross their legs or arms are signaling that they are closed to the speaker. Or they could just be chilly. An open body position indicates openness to the speaker's point. Leaning forward indicates interest; leaning back indicates disinterest. Leaning back and clasping hands above or behind the head indicates extreme confidence or triumph, while leaning forward with hands under the legs or under the table indicates insecurity. Or it indicates that your hands are cold. If you read the books and practice observation, these indicators and others like them will soon become obvious to you in every meeting you have.

Another great benefit of being able to read body language is in communicating with children, especially teenagers. Teenagers are sometimes hard to understand because they are less verbally open than younger children. With teenagers, sometimes "F-you" means, "I need a hug." Sometimes "You don't trust me," means, "I need more rules." Sometimes "I'm okay, leave me alone," means, "I'm okay, leave me alone." But teenagers are very open with their body language. Learning a few keys will help you decipher where your teenager is coming from.

For example, a teenager who wears his hair in his face is hiding and/or escaping from something. This can indicate low self-esteem or a desire to avoid the present situation. If a teenager is slumped in the car or chair, turned away from the driver/parent, this may mean they don't want to talk. However, if their IPod earplugs are not in their ears or if they interact with the radio or do something else inconsistent with wanting to be isolated, it shows that they may want to talk. You may gently inquire, "How's it going?" But approach with caution— the teenage species can be unpredictable.

The Six Classic Involuntary Signals

Talking through your hand(s)	Lying or hiding something
Arms or legs crossed	Closed to ideas
Leaning in	Interested
Leaning out, arms crossed	Disinterested
Leaning back, hands behind head	Confident
"Choking on words"	The speaker does not believe what they are saying

A fundamental understanding of six obvious gestures is the beginning of understanding body language. Be warned, this is only the tip of the iceberg when it comes to understanding body language. Understanding body language requires an understanding of all of the elements of a situation. For example, if you see somebody wearing only a t-shirt on a chilly fall day and their arms are crossed in front of them, this probably means they are cold (not disinterested). To truly understand body language, you must understand all of the signals being emitted, which may be internally contrary.

Talking Through a Hand or Fingers

Most people have trouble lying. People who can lie without showing it are dangerous. To understand them you would have to go deep into understanding body language. However, there are signals you can count on with most people.

Mary is behind deadline on a project for her manager. She needs to finish by the end of the day but she is not sure she will have enough time. She knows she will be staying through lunch and still may not finish it.

Mary remembers that he co-worker, Jerry, owes her a favor. She helped him out in a similar situation a month ago, so she decides to go to Jerry's office and ask for his help. Jerry is generally helpful, so she is optimistic.

Mary explains her plight to Jerry. Jerry wants to be helpful and he knows he owes her a favor. He also knows that he is scheduled to play golf that afternoon for the first time all summer. He answers the question vaguely. "I have an appointment this afternoon" he says. "I would really like to help, but I am not available." Mary responds, not suspecting anything, "Oh, who is your appointment with?"

Now Jerry is stuck. If he tells the truth, Mary will know he is letting her down for the sake of a golf game. He also knows that if she is aware his appointment is for golf, she will probably insist that he help her (as he knows he should). But Jerry wants to play golf, so he responds with a lie. "I am meeting with Smith, from Acme." As he lies, his index finger and the finger next to it briefly rise to his lips.

Mary understands body language and she understands this signal. Covering your mouth while you speak often means that you are not telling the truth. The generally honest person involuntarily tries to "block" the lie with one or more fingers or their whole hand. This gesture can be obvious or more subtle. It can involve one finger briefly touching the lips of the speaker or it can involve a whole hand placed over the bottom half of the face. Some speakers will even put one finger to their mouth as they draw a breath before they make a dishonest statement.

This gesture, by the way, generally comes from people who are normally honest. People who are habitual liars have learned to control this gesture.

Mary is now fully informed and can decide what to do with the information. She knows that Jerry is avoiding helping her for a reason he doesn't want to disclose.

If you see somebody talking through their hand, listen carefully to their statement. It is probably not true. This is a great way to see if someone is bluffing during a negotiation. If you see this gesture, figure of why the person would be "lying" and you will start to understand what they are thinking.

Arms or Legs Crossed

When you see someone cross their arms or legs in front of them, this indicates that they are closed to the idea you presented. If they are leaning back and crossing their arms or legs, this indicates that they are disinterested. In the starkest terms, the person who is closed to your ideas has decided that you are wrong. The person who is disinterested in your ideas has decided the ideas are not important to them.

This gesture, like most body language, can be obvious or subtle. If you are selling or otherwise trying to persuade somebody across the table and you see them cross their arms, this indicates you are losing them.

If this signal is a surprise to you, think back to something you just said or did that may have been received negatively. Could they have misunderstood what you said? Are they wrongly predisposed to being closed to your ideas (e.g. prejudicial against them because of something they don't know)? Can you tell them something that will draw them back to you?

I experienced a perfect example of this many years ago at a market in Italy, haggling over the price of a gift for my brother. I was trying to buy a tie and the list price was $15. I was offering $5 and the seller was down to $10. As we continued to talk, I noticed his arms were folded across his chest and his face was stern. At that point, my friend arrived and I updated him on the situation. He said, "how about if we buy 5 ties for $25?" The seller's hands slowly unfolded from his chest as he stepped forward. He still had a scowl on his face but I know, now, in retrospect, that my friend's offer re-gained his interest. We continue to haggle. We ended up buying 6 ties for $30 and finished our gift shopping early.

Again, it is important to note that these gestures are sometimes subtle. Here, I am talking about crossing of arms but it could be a person sitting with their ankles crossed or having their hands clasped together in front of them. Even crossed hands can indicate a problem, if the rest of the body language is consistent.

The key is to read the person's entire body position as being closed or open. Open body position means they are open to your ideas. Closed body position means they are closed or disinterested.

Leaning In or Out

If somebody's position is forward or back, this indicates interest or disinterest. A person leaning forward is trying to get "closer" to your words because of their increased interest. A person leaning back is trying to get "farther" from your words because they are less interested or, sometimes, afraid of them.

Sometimes this manifests itself in a dramatic way. I remember having a discussion with the three owners of a closely held corporation. The corporation was in trouble and they were meeting with us to discuss the possibility of bankruptcy. They weren't certain they wanted to declare bankruptcy. The operating partner (without money) wanted to continue the business. The financial partner (who had been funding the company) wanted to stop funding the company and declare bankruptcy. The third partner was less involved, undecided and was listening. His decision would be critical. Over the course of the discussion, the partners determined that going forward would require an immediate injection of $50,000 in cash. As soon as this number was determined and the third partner had endorsed the addition of more capital, the funding partner suddenly shot back in his chair away from the table. He hit the wall so hard that he also hit his head. This gesture was an involuntary response to his own realization that he was about to put $50,000 more of his own money into this company.

There is an interesting theory...

Of course, this is an extreme example. The usual signal (when sitting) is a movement of the shoulder and head back and away from the table. When standing, you will see a step backwards, with either one or both feet. There is an interesting theory that says that interest can be created by inducing someone to lean forward. You can do this by speaking softly so they have to lean forward to hear or by putting something in front of them to read, in such a position that they are forced to lean forward to read it. I don't really subscribe to this theory but I have never seen anything disproving it.

Leaning in can be dramatic, but is usually more subtle. Watch for a tip of the chin forward. Watch for movement of the hands forward on the table. Any gesture that moves the individual closer to you indicates that you have hit the right spot. This is what they are interested in. This is what you can use to your advantage.

Leaning Back, Hands Behind Head

If somebody leans back and puts their hand behind their head, this means that they are feeling triumphant or confident in their position. It is an unguarded position. They feel invulnerable. They simply relax and open up their body completely by putting their hands behind their head.

Often, you will see this gesture after the other side makes a major concession. It is more important to note whether someone takes this position after they say something. If they do, that exemplifies that they are self-assured and satisfied with their position. If somebody tells you this is their last offer and then leans back with their hands on their head, you can be pretty sure that it is their last offer. They have nothing left to lose and no more retreat to make, so they are relaxing.

You can take advantage of this gesture. It is an easy gesture to fake (so beware). I sometimes use this gesture myself to signal the other side that I am confident in what I just said. In poker, using this gesture at the right time can make somebody think you are not bluffing. Beware though, because it will only work once in a given poker game.

Choking on Words

Choking on words, sputtering or hesitation in saying something usually means that the speaker does not believe what he is saying (or at least lacks confidence in it). This is different than lying. This usually comes about when somebody is making a forceful statement either about their own position or about the future.

Before a particular hockey season started, I heard the coach talking to the press. As he said, "I believe we will win the state tournament this year" he choked on the word "win". It was a subtle hesitation, just a stumble. However, I recognized that he didn't really believe that they could win the state tournament. (As it turned out, the team did not win.)

Ronald Reagan made one of the great, historic statements of the twentieth century when he said "Mr. Gorbachev, tear down that wall." This was high-theatre in a tense time. In one of the Ronald Reagan biographical documentaries, they play a larger excerpt from that same speech. Interestingly, Ronald Reagan stumbled on his first attempt at the sentence. What he actually said was "Mr. Gorbachev" (pause) "Mr. Gorbachev, tear down that wall." This pause leads me to believe that Ronald Reagan knew that Mr. Gorbachev wasn't going to be persuaded to tear down the wall by anything the President of the United States said in a speech. However, being the accomplished actor that he was, President Reagan recovered from his stumble and redelivered the line in one piece, creating a quote that has been replayed millions of times around the world.

This gesture can also manifest by drawing breath at unusual times, yawns in the middle of a sentence or even a full sudden stop. Statements that are delivered with confidence are delivered smoothly and directly. If your speaker does not believe in what they are saying, only the most accomplished or well-rehearsed speaker can cover it up.

Whenever somebody interrupts themself or stumbles over their own words, take a hard look at what they are saying. It is possible that they themselves do not believe in what they are saying or do not believe their words will have the desired effect.

SKILL #2
Interviewing and Listening

Interviewing and interrogation make up the active side of listening. If you are uncomfortable asking deep probing questions, get over it. The answers to these questions are your best source of information about your counterpart and the straightest road to good results.

There are three broad types of questions. Information-gathering questions help you understand the positions and motivation of the other side. Strategic questions help you gain commitments from the other side that will help you later in the game. Crossroads questions simultaneously present a buying signal and a threat to walk away, and they help motivate an opponent to agree with you.

Information-Gathering Questions

The most important part of early negotiations is gathering information from your counterpart. You must discover their needs and wants, the issues important to them, and much other information. The best way to do this is by asking questions. Information-gathering questions are usually open-ended. This allows the other side to talk and get comfortable while you listen and get educated. Education is a good thing.

Open-ended Questions

Open-ended questions can be used to gather information, both about the deal and about your counterpart. They permit a broad range of answers. Open-ended questions include, "What did you like about . . . ?" and, "What was your reaction to . . . ?" These questions are useful in getting the other side to share things that are important to them without you setting the parameters. These questions help build rapport, because your counterpart gets to speak their mind and you get to be a good listener (people like good listeners). Open-ended questions can be used effectively to help determine your counterpart's motivational level.

One great open-ended question is, "What do you like about our product?" This gets the other side talking about how great you are and thinking in concordance with you. You can also ask about your product's weaknesses early on. Both of these questions give you insight into what is motivating the other side. For example, if Betty says that one of your strengths is that her boss has worked with you for years then personal recognition (Level III motivation) may motivate her. You will then focus your discussion on reliability, the long-term relationship, and how staying with you will not be a mistake.

On the other hand, if someone says that your strengths are innovation and new direction then that person may be operating on Level IV (status). You will then focus your efforts on how the product will make that person stand out, look good, and become a star. We'll discuss specific motivation levels in chapter 5.

Open-ended questions encourage the responder to wander and elaborate. This is a good thing when you are gathering information early in negotiations. However, don't use open-ended questions when you are near the endgame or when you feel you have momentum. Open-ended questions introduce an element of randomness into the discussion. You don't want randomness when you are about to close a deal. On the other hand, if things are going south, asking an open-ended question might turn things in your favor. For example, when discussions are headed toward deadlock, I often ask, "Do you see any solutions?" This question gets the other side talking and often reveals something new that gets the deal done.

Direct Questions

Direct questions are most useful at the beginning and the end of the negotiation. At the beginning of the negotiation the risk is lower, because you need to know certain answers or you need to know if further discussion is worthwhile. Questions like this include, "Can you produce ten thousand widgets in sixty days?" and, "How big of an order are you expecting to place with me (or the competition) on this project?" Direct questions are also useful at closing. They are less risky here because you usually know the answers and the direct questions are necessary to get the deal finished. Questions like this include, "If I can meet your price point, do we have a deal?" and, "Is this your best price?" These are questions designed to close the deal.

Direct questions usually work very well when the answer is important but not likely to change. "Are you concerned with our insurance level?" This is a risk-free question, because either they are okay with it or you can buy more insurance. However, you need to know the answer to properly price the deal. Use direct questions to qualify the other side: "Do you have the capacity to produce one million widgets a week?" This is an important and risk-free question, because they either have the capacity or they don't. If they don't, the deal is off, but it's better to find out early. Ask qualifying questions early on. You should actually know the answers to most of your qualifying questions before your first face-to-face meeting.

Direct questions are both valuable and risky. With a direct question you are asking specifically for information you want without allowing your counterpart any wiggle room to avoid a direct answer. This is risky because sometimes you won't get the answer you want. Direct questions are questions that specifically ask for certain information. Examples include: "Do you have the authority to approve this transaction?" "If I produce this in red, will you buy it today?" "What can I do to get your business?"

Indirect Questions

Indirect questions are best used in the early stages, when you're engaged with important deal terms that are likely to be negotiated, like price. If you are in the first meeting and ask, "What is your best price per widget?" (a direct question) you put the other side in a position where they must commit to a figure that you will want them to change later. Once committed, change is difficult. Instead, the early meeting question might be, "How much are you looking to get per widget?" This gives the other side the chance to ask for a higher price but still have the freedom to withdraw to a position you prefer. Consider the following examples.

Buyer: What is your best price for this car?
Seller: $23,900, as is.
Buyer: That is more than I want to pay. How about $21,500?

Now the seller has to stand firm or, by changing, admit that $23,900 is not the "best price." Here is an alternative scenario:

Buyer: How much are you looking to get for this car?
Seller: $24,900, as is.
Buyer: That is more than I want to pay. I'm thinking more along the lines of $21,000.
Seller [who can now gracefully reduce the earlier price]: I

can't really go that low. I can go to $23,900, but not much lower.

Buyer: How about $23,000?

Seller: Deal.

Another version of the indirect question is asking one question to get the answer to a different question. This sometimes allows you to get information without offending the other side or without revealing your own position. One of my favorites is, "Where are you staying?" The answer will reveal how much someone spent on a hotel room and, in turn, teach you something about the person's financial position. (By the way, if you are asked this question, the best answer is "downtown." Follow-up questions about your hotel tend to be awkward and are usually not asked.)

Compound Questions

Compound questions contain a question within a question. An example is, "How was your flight?" which also includes the question, "Did you drive from Chicago or did you fly?" Compound questions often seem nonthreatening but the underlying answer can provide valuable information. The classic compound question is, "Are you happy with our company's performance?" If the answer is yes, then that can later be used to remind your opponent of their happiness with the performance of the product, the delivery, and the price.

The downside of compound questions is that they can lead to wasted time and false impressions. For example, the buyer may be happy with your company's product but not with the delivery schedule. However, the person may not bring up the delivery schedule unless specifically asked about it. So by asking only the question, "Are you happy with our company's performance?" then you might be providing your customer an opportunity to avoid confrontation while you lose an opportunity to discover a problem. If you really want information, it is better to use a direct question.

Leading Questions

You can control the range of answers by tailoring the questions. For example, to gain an admission (that you know the other side must eventually make), use leading questions. Leading questions generally limit the answers to yes, no, or I don't know. Open-ended questions work well when you do not know what the answers are or when you want to get the other person talking. Open-ended questions are great for gathering information. But it is the leading questions that limit possible responses. Between these two types of questions are direct questions, indirect questions, and compound questions.

Leading questions take the responder directly to the answer the interrogator wants to hear. For example, "You are staying at the Marriot, correct?" The open-ended question is, "How is your hotel?" The direct question is, "Are you staying at the Marriot?" A compound question is, "Are you staying at the Marriot or the Hilton?" Another form of compound question is, "How do you like the Marriot?" This form contains the unstated assumption that you are staying at the Marriot, so any answer like "fine" also answers the question. Each of these forms is useful for different things. Prepare your questions in advance and you will be in control of the negotiation.

Leading questions are most effective at the beginning of a discussion or as a closing tool at the end. You can use leading questions to quickly cover the early, noncontroversial points of interest. Leading questions establish the foundation for later discussions. For example:

"You are still happy with our widgets?"
"There were no problems with that last big shipment?"
"You have a budget of $80,000 a month for this project?"
"You know that the union has not had a raise in seven years?"

As a closing tool, leading questions are also very effective. Use points established in earlier discussions as leading questions to create a closing syllogism. "Your target audience is youth hockey players, right?" (Response is yes.) "We reach youth hockey more effectively than anyone else, right?" (Yes.) "So, you should advertise with us, right?" (Yes.) "Did you decide to take the full-page ad six times per year or twelve times per year [compound question]?" (Six times.) "So we will set you up with the full page, six times per year?" (Yes.) Deal done.

Leading questions limit the range of answers. Usually they lead to a single answer, with the alternative to disagree. They are efficient, but should not be abused. Use too many in a row and your counterpart will feel manipulated and maybe even start to push back. Notice in the closing syllogism (above) that we inserted a compound question to break up the series.

Types of Information-Gathering Questions

Open-ended	Early stages Gather information about the deal Gather information about your counterpart Determine your counterpart's motivation level Get your counterpart talking Example: "How is your hotel?"
Direct	Early, end, and closing stages Situations that are not likely to change Qualify negotiation before proceeding to negotiate. Example: "Are you staying at the Marriot?"
Indirect	Early stages To get answers to other questions without asking directly. Example: "Are you staying at a hotel?"
Compound	Question within a question, used at any stage Example: "Are you staying at the Marriot or the Hilton?"
Leading	Early on and at closing To gain an admission Example: "You are staying at the Marriot, correct?"

Strategic Questions

Strategic questions are critical to negotiations and are too often ignored. Strategic questions are the difference between playing chess and playing checkers. Chess masters play many moves ahead of the board. Strategic questions enable you to gain positional commitments from the other side before they even realize they're committing.

Strategic questions are very important in complex negotiations. Anytime you are negotiating with the expectation of having multiple meetings (in other words, not closing at this meeting) you should be thinking of asking strategic questions. These are the same types of questions as information-gathering questions; however, these questions will be asked differently when they are part of your strategy. Strategic questions help you to find the other side's position and help you position yourself for the end game.

I used to negotiate contracts for medical clinics against health insurance companies or "health maintenance organizations" (HMOs). In my home state of Minnesota, four HMOs dominate the healthcare market. Most medical clinics rely on these four HMOs (also called "payors") to cumulatively pay 90 percent of their revenue. Medical clinics must negotiate contracts with each of these HMOs to become part of the network. Often, clinics think they have no leverage and simply accept a payor's offer without negotiating. But there is another side to the story.

Each HMO competes with the others to sell their program to larger clinics. In order to compete, HMOs must have complete coverage throughout the state, both in terms of geography and medical specialty. In other words, every clinic an HMO covers must have access to an ear, nose, and throat specialist (ENT), a general surgeon, and every other medical specialty, all within convenient driving distance. I have negotiated with HMOs on behalf of such specialists.

A shortage of doctors in some practice specialties creates leverage for the specialists. Typically, a midsize city will have a single dominant clinic for a given specialty. In the same market, there may be 500,000 lives that the HMO wants to insure. The HMO must provide full access to medical care in order to sign up major clinics in the area. The specialists, on the other hand, are usually very busy because theirs is the only such clinic in town. This situation gives clinics with specialty services negotiation leverage in two ways. The HMO cannot be secure in its local offering without signing up, for example, the only ENT clinic in town. The ENT clinic, on the other hand, has more business than it can handle, so they are very secure about their future business prospects.

Because they typically provide an important part of the clinic's business, the HMO often comes to the first meeting with confidence and sometimes arrogance. At that meeting, my team uses strategic questions to seek a commitment from the HMO negotiator, but first we have to ensure they have the authority to negotiate outside normal parameters. We make it clear that we expect to get a better deal than they usually give. So the negotiator must admit either (1) that they don't have extraordinary authority or (2) that they are willing to give us a better deal. Any other direct response threatens the deal, which they certainly don't have the authority to do. They usually are not prepared to answer this direct challenge.

Negotiators usually avoid answering the challenge by offering, instead, one of several standard arguments based on either fairness or leverage. I've heard all of these arguments before, but I still listen very carefully. The negotiator's tone, choice of statements, body language, and level of emotion teach me how he or she reacts when their own comfort zone is threatened. I then use this information to gauge the negotiator's reactions later, when we are in less familiar territory.

At the right time, I will call the negotiator back to the question by asking something like, "Are you telling me that you are not willing to consider giving us a deal that is outside your normal range?" Now, the negotiator will either admit that they have the authority to do so or tell me that I must talk to their boss. Either answer they give is fine with me, because then we are soon talking with the decision maker about getting a better deal.

In the meantime, I have also learned something about my opponent. I know how they react when uncomfortable. I know whether they are sincere, whether they are direct or indirect, and I know the motivational level they are operating on. I also know how well prepared they are. All of this helps me as we move forward in the negotiation.

Note that my opponent could have simply answered the question as, "Yes, I have the authority," or, "No, I don't." (This answer comes out eventually.) If the negotiator answers directly like this, I learn very little about them that I can use later. When I hear such a direct answer, I know I have a well-prepared and sophisticated negotiator on the other side.

This is a good example of strategic questioning. We tried to gain a commitment from the negotiator that he had the ability to make a deal outside of the normal range. His commitment would deprive him of a whole category of arguments based on historical practices, their budget, and such arguments as, "What if we paid everyone that much?" This positioning creates major advantages because it focuses the endgame on, "What is our value to you?" instead of, "What are you paying the other guys?" Of course, if your value is less than the other guys, you will want to employ a strategy that includes you as part of the pack.

Compound and indirect questions can also be used strategically. These are tricky, because they often contain a question within a question. This makes them useful when you are trying to get an answer that might otherwise be difficult to obtain. If you want to know whether your client's insurance business might be up for bid, you can ask about the insurance agent, Fred. If the client speaks poorly about Fred, then you might conclude that the business is in play.

"Positioning," in the art of negotiation, means putting yourself in a place where you can direct the negotiation exactly where you want it to go. By asking the right strategic questions, you can put yourself and your opposition in the position that is to your best advantage.

A good example of positioning comes from my days as a radio-time seller. Radio stations make money selling commercial time to advertisers. Advertisers, generally, choose where to buy their advertising based on the audiences of the radio station. A radio audience can be parsed in many different ways. For example, the same radio station can be ranked first among 18- to 34-year-old women listeners; third among 25- to 54-year-old men; and tenth in all listeners age 12 plus. There are literally dozens of these categories in the standard audience ratings.

To effectively sell radio time, it is important to position the potential advertiser through strategic questions. Upon learning what the advertiser is looking for, the seller can point out how the station's audience matches the needs of the advertiser, tailoring the presentation to cast the station in the best possible light. Here is an example of a visit by a seller to a local jewelry store.

> Radio-Time Seller (after preliminary discussion): So tell me, who are your customers?
>
> Jewelry Store: We get people from all over the western suburbs.
>
> Seller: This is pretty nice stuff. You obviously have high-end clientele.
>
> Jeweler: Yes, we do. Mostly incomes of $100,000 plus, I would guess.
>
> Seller: Who usually makes the decision—the man or the woman?

Jeweler: It's about the same of each.

Seller: So you would like to reach an audience with incomes of $100,000?

Jeweler: Yes, that's the type of people we are trying to reach.

Seller: Well, are you aware that our radio station has more listeners with incomes of $100,000 than any station in the market?

Jeweler: I did not know that.

[The discussion would continue into closing.]

Here you can see the use of questions to *position* the potential advertiser. The seller knew the station's largest audience was incomes of $100,000 plus. The seller also knew that the jeweler would want to attract people of this income (that is why the seller called on the jeweler in the first place). So the seller positioned the negotiation to the point in which it would be illogical for the jewelry store buyer to say no. Why would anyone not want to buy advertising on a radio station that reaches more of the prime customer demographic than any other station? Of course, the match is not always perfect.

Seller: So you would like to reach an audience with incomes of $100,000 plus?

Jeweler: We don't use radio advertising to reach our existing customers. We actually want to reach a younger demographic and create new customers for life.

Seller: And these would be the people who have the potential for high income?

Jeweler: Yes. They might be in their twenties or thirties and maybe making $50,000 per year.

Seller: Well, our station is third in the 18-to-34 age group but we have far more listeners with college degrees than the two stations that are slightly ahead of us.

As you can see, your counterparts do not always go exactly where you want to position them. However, if you are well prepared and know your opponent, you can position the negotiation to your advantage. Strategic questions are also very useful in the endgame. "Would you like the car in red or in white?" is one example of a strategic closing question. Closing questions are discussed in chapter 7.

Crossroads Questions

Crossroads questions combine a buying signal and a threat to walk away. When I represent a buyer, I sometimes ask, "Is this your best price?" (or "best deal") near the end of a negotiation but before committing to the deal. This positions the seller so they know the sale has probably been made, unless they get too greedy on the "best (offered) price." Often, you will get a nice concession here, conditioned on your closing the deal. You can employ strategic questions in the endgame to affirm your negotiations, leading to a crossroads question and, ultimately, to closing. For example:

Ted: To confirm, you can deliver 10,000 widgets per month?
Ed: No problem.
Ted: And you can them deliver to all seven stores?
Ed: Yes.
Ted: And shipping is included?
Ed: Yes.
Ted: And you want $50 per widget?
Ed: Yes.
Ted: Is that your best price?
Ed: [silent]
Ted: [silent]
Ed: If you can sign now, I can come down to $48 per widget, but it's killing me.
Ted: Outstanding. Where is the paperwork?

"Is that your best price?" is a crossroads question because it presents two contradictory positions to the other side.

Asking questions about price is a buying signal, but asking if the price offered is their final position carries a tacit walk-away threat. If the seller (or buyer) has room to move, they will be motivated to do so by this question.

"Do you have the authority to negotiate outside normal parameters?" is a crossroads question. The question carries the dual implications that we want to do a deal with you (a buying signal) but only if it's better than normal (a threat to walk away).

There are some crossroads questions that need to be asked early in the negotiations. These include qualifying questions like, "Are you the decision maker?" or, "If you get the job, are you willing to move to Phoenix?" Some crossroads questions are best saved for the late stages. "If I meet your price, is that the last issue?" is a great closer. "If I fly out to see you next week, can we finalize this deal?" gains a commitment from the other side in return for your time and travel. It puts you at or near the endgame at your next meeting.

Listen to The Answers

Artful questioning can be the difference between reaching a deal or not. Questions are worthless unless you listen effectively. The first requirement of being a strong listener is that you listen actively. Focus on your counterpart's words and body language. Do not compose your answer until your opponent has finished speaking. If your counterpart makes a point that you want to respond to but keeps talking, it is okay to politely interrupt them to respond to that point. However, do not compose your response to that point while your opponent continues talking. If you do, you may miss vital information, including nonverbal signs.

It helps to remind yourself that the point of any negotiation is to get your counterpart to do what you want them to do. You are trying to motivate them to reach an agreement with you. It is very difficult for you to focus on what your opponent is saying if you are taking notes. I usually do not take notes, except very sparingly. However, I believe in the value of notes. Therefore, in a meeting of any significance, I want to have a second person with me to take notes. This note taker should not be writing every word said, but should be noting the key points, including any hidden concessions or body language.

> *The point of all negotiation is to get your counterpart to do what you want them to do.*
> *You must motivate them to reach an agreement with you.*

Hidden Concessions

Hidden concessions can be a gold mine for a strong listener. A hidden concession arises between the lines of a negotiator's statements. The most famous principle of hidden concessions is that "a dollar stated is a dollar on the table." This means that if somebody says, "My client is not willing to pay $20,000," it really means that the client is willing to pay $20,000. However, the most valuable hidden concessions are usually more subtle than that.

Jack and Steve are real estate brokers. Jack is trying to sell a house to Steve's client. Steve wants to pay $525,000 and Jack wants him to pay $550,000. After Steve explains his version of the comps in the marketplace, Jack says, "That doesn't matter, my client is stuck on $550,000." The hidden concession here is that Jack agrees with Steve's analysis of the market, and thinks the house is worth only $525,000, but he still wants Steve's client to pay $550,000. Jack will never say, "I agree that it is only worth $525,000 but I want you to pay $550,000." Rather, he will either claim the point is irrelevant or change the subject. When you see your opponent avoid something that clearly is relevant (like comps in a real estate sale) then you know that they agree with your point.

Hidden concessions are often discovered by listening to what your counterpart is *not* saying. For example, a person who claims that "nobody's widget is faster than ours" or "more powerful" or "more economical," etc., means that there are other widgets on the market that are just as fast (or powerful or economical, etc.). If not, he would say, "Our widget is the fastest."

Rather than concede a negative point, a good seller will redirect you to their strengths. Walk into any electronics store and ask for a Sony TV. If they don't sell Sony, they will direct you to the brand that they do sell rather than just tell you, "You can't get a Sony here, so you should go home." The same is true with business negotiations.

Hidden concessions are often signaled by a few magic words. If you hear "yes, but . . ." they are conceding with your point and at the same time following it with an argument. If you hear "that's not unreasonable, but . . ." they are agreeing to the statement they label as "not unreasonable." Hidden concessions are often spoken quickly, in the preamble to another argument. If you do not listen carefully, you will miss them. Hidden concessions are very real. You need to actively listen for them. Once the hidden concession is made, you can use it to your advantage as the negotiation proceeds.

A hidden concession provides knowledge you can use in your strategic model. Almost always, the knowledge came from a hidden concession, and like revenge, it is a dish best served cold. Think about our real estate example (above). . . .

Buyer's Agent: The comps we've just reviewed clearly show that the top end for this house is $525,000. My client is offering $525,000.

Seller's Agent: I don't care what the comps say; my client won't sell for anything less than $550,000. [Seller's Agent just made a hidden concession that the comps are reasonable and he has no argument against them.]

Buyer's Agent [confronting the hidden concession]: So you agree that my comps are reasonable and your client is just being stubborn?

Seller's Agent: I didn't agree that your comps are reasonable, I just said it doesn't matter what the comps are. My client's price is $550,000. [The buyer's confrontation has forced him to defend his statement.]

Buyer's Agent: So your client will demand $550,000 even if the reasonable value of the house is $525,000?

Seller's Agent: Yes.

Buyer's Agent: Well then, he will never sell the house; certainly not to any client of mine. We are going to look elsewhere.

Seller's Agent: Okay. Thank you very much for your time.

You see here that immediately confronting the hidden concession required the seller's agent to deny the concession; this eventually put the seller's agent into an unreasonable position. The result of the unreasonable position was that no deal happened, which was bad for everyone. The buyer's agent could have handled this matter another way.

Buyer's Agent: The comps clearly show that the high-end range for this house is $525,000. My client is offering $525,000. I think your client should take the offer.

Seller's Agent: I don't care what the comps say. My client won't sell for a penny less than $550,000. [Making a hidden concession that the house is worth $525,000.]

At this point, the buyer's agent knows that the seller's agent believes the $525,000 price is reasonable. He is stuck at $550,000. This means that the seller's agent is trying to get more out of the sale or that the seller actually is unreasonable. The hope is to eventually get to the higher price. However, the seller's agent doesn't confront the hidden concession directly.

Buyer's Agent: So your client thinks the house is worth $550,000?

Seller's Agent: Yes.

Buyer's Agent: Can you please explain why the buyer thinks that?

Seller's Agent: Well, this buyer really needs to get $550,000 to pay off the current mortgage and use the difference as a down payment on a new house.

This is an important piece of information. This is the real reason the house is priced at $550,000. Now the buyer's agent, using strategic questions, can attack the seller's math. The buyer's agent can ask questions about the cost of the new house, the desired down-payment amount, and the realtor's commission. This puts the discussion in the realm of arithmetic.

Buyer's Agent: Alright, so how much does the buyer need for a down payment?

Seller's Agent: About $100,000. [Here is another hidden concession, with use of the word "about." *About* indicates it is not a precise number. It is the seller's goal, not something the seller "must have."]

Buyer's Agent: So he owes $450,000 on this house? [Buyer's Agent knows from researching public records that seller only owes about $420,000.]

Seller's Agent: Well, no. He only owes about $420,000 but you have to think about commission as well. Combined, our commission is going to be about $25,000.

Buyer's Agent: Okay, so even with $25,000 in commissions the buyer will still get $100,000 if the house sells for $545,000. And, if we knock a point off of the commission we can get the buyer about $100,000 at $540,000. Right?

Seller's Agent: Yes.

Buyer's Agent: So we're only $15,000 apart. If you can get the seller to get by with $92,500, I think I can get the buyer to split the difference and come in at $532,500. This seems like a fair price.

The buyer's agent, through proper planning, was fully aware of the arithmetic of the deal. All comparable sales in the marketplace were researched and the offer was a fair price based on these comps. Once the buyer's agent picked up on the first hidden concession—the seller's agent agreed that the comps were reasonable—it was obvious that some simple arithmetic was going to get the deal done.

Two other principles become apparent in this example. The first principle is the importance of research (to be explored in chapter 6). In the above example, the buyer's agent was able to negotiate $18,000 off the purchase price, and get the deal done. Because of pre-negotiation research, the buyer's agent knew how much the seller owed on the house, the real estate commission, and the value of the house. Without this research, it is likely that no deal would have been done, certainly not at the price the buyer was able to negotiate.

The other principle apparent in this example is the value of strategic questions. In the second example, the buyer's agent uses strategic questions (in this case, leading questions) to take the seller's agent down the path to the ultimate purchase price. The buyer's agent knew the answers to the questions. However, in going directly to confrontation, as in the first example, the agreement would have never been reached.

Now, let's look at another hidden concession based on the same example. What if the seller's agent began the conversation as follows:

Buyer's Agent: The comps clearly show the value of this house between $520,000 and $530,000. We are offering in the middle of that range. [The hidden concession is that the buyer thinks $530,000 is a reasonable value for the house even though they are only offering $525,000.]

Seller's Agent: I don't care what the comps say. My client is stuck on $550,000. [Also making a hidden concession that the reasonable value of the house is between $520,000 and $530,000.]

Now, assume the same conversation took place as in our second example. The buyer's agent does a good job of asking strategic questions and employing arithmetic to get to the following point:

Buyer's Agent: If the seller can get by with $92,500, we would be willing to split the difference at $532,500. This seems like a fair price.

Seller's Agent:That's not really splitting the difference because you already put $530,000 on the table. Let's look at $535,000.

Buyer's Agent: I think I can talk the buyer into $535,000.

At this point, the seller's agent is not going to let the house go for the $2,500 difference so they do the deal at $535,000. The buyer's agent made a hidden concession that cost the client (buyer) $2,500. Hidden concessions are one of the keys to successful negotiating.

> **Hidden Concessions are Gold**
>
> *Take advantage of the other side's hidden concessions and you gain advantages for your side. Picking up on hidden concessions often enables you to get a deal done.*

The other side of the coin is that your own hidden concession can be damaging. Be very careful if you make a hidden concession that you are doing it deliberately. In the third example above, the buyer's agent gave the reasonable range and made a hidden concession. In some cases, you may want to provide information to the other side that you want them to have. In the third example, the buyer's agent may have felt it was necessary to signal the $535,000 so the seller's agent knew that the buyer wasn't entrenched at $525,000. Likewise, the seller's agent's hidden concession that the comps were reasonable (made by not arguing against the comps) could have been done intentionally to make sure the buyer did not walk away over the difference between $525,000 and $550,000.

Hidden concessions are a major part of any negotiating strategy. By understanding the other side's hidden concessions, and by judiciously making hidden concessions of your own, you can often move the negotiation toward agreement. Remember, the goal of any negotiation is to reach an agreement that is acceptable to you. Hidden concessions between the parties are outwardly stating the range that might be mutually acceptable to both of them.

The physical act of listening is fairly difficult. It really requires concentration more than anything else. Concentration is easier if you really care about what the other person is saying, so you need to understand, really understand, what your opponent says. What the opponent says is, ultimately, more important in reaching a deal than what you say. You need to care about what they say.

Buying Signals

Another form of hidden concessions is a buying signal. A buying signal can be made by either a seller or a buyer and does not necessarily deal with price. A buying signal is a statement that reveals you are interested in moving the negotiations of the deal to the next level.

The most obvious examples of buying signals come from a buyer, the strongest being about price. For example, car dealers know they have strong potential to make a sale as soon as the potential customer asks about costs. This means the customer wants the car, if the price is right. Such buying signals come any time a potential buyer asks a question that moves the negotiations to the next level. For example, "Does this dress come in blue?" really means that the customer would be interested in buying the dress if it came in blue. In the dating realm, at the end of the night, asking, "Would you like to come up for a cup of coffee?" may signal interest in taking the relationship to a new level. Someone who lists the price of an object on Craigslist as "$150 or best offer" is signaling that they will take just about anything reasonable to get rid of the object.

You need to listen well to hear buying signals. For instance, in the dating example above, a poor listener may have simply said, "No thanks, it's too late at night for me to have a cup of coffee," and would have missed the opportunity presented. People who want to buy the $150 object on Craigslist may overpay for it if they don't understand that "or best offer" is a buying signal that indicates the seller wants to move this deal directly to closing. If you get a buying signal, you should take the negotiation to the next level. When you hear, "Does this dress come in blue?" you no longer need to talk about the designer or the style or the good value of the dress. Your buyer has already accepted those points. You've won those points. Now, just figure out a way to get that dress in blue and you have a deal.

Car sellers are great at recognizing buying signals. This is because they are very good listeners. When they hear someone ask about financing, they stop talking about the power or MPGs of the car. They move very quickly to getting you into their closing room to talk about financing.

This works not just with cars. If any buyer asks about price, payments, financing, or anything that has to do with money, they are sending a strong buying signal. They are ready to accept the terms of the deal if the price is right.

To listen well, you need to recognize buying signals. Once you successfully recognize buying signals your results will improve dramatically.

Active listening takes practice. Like reading body language, it is an acquired skill and can be learned. Practice it all the time. Practice it with your family and co-workers and you will often find them pleasantly surprised that someone is paying so much attention to them. This is a positive by-product of being an active listener.

The first step in active listening is to actually look at the person who is talking. One trick is to not look the person directly in the eye, but to look at a spot in the middle of their forehead. This enables you to watch the other person without being distracted by an uncomfortable staring contest. At the same time, make sure you are watching the person's body language. Reading body language is an important aspect of active listening.

By asking the right questions and listening to the answers, you can find out a great deal about your counterpart's motivations. Once you have this information, you are well on your way to a positive conclusion.

Listen to your opponent carefully.

What your opponent says is more important than what you say.

SKILL #3
Getting Ready (Preparation)

The object of preparation is to create a full understanding of the negotiation in advance. You don't fully understand the negotiation until you can predict with some degree of certainty the course the negotiation will take and, within a reasonably tight range, predict the outcome you expect. This predicted outcome must be supported by an understanding of three things: (1) the other side's best alternative to a negotiated agreement (BATNA), (2) the other side's motivation (as well as your own), and (3) the other side's goals (as well as your own). Even though these things may change over the course of negotiation, you aren't prepared to start negotiation until you have reasonable certainty about all three points. Without knowing these three points, you cannot control the negotiation.

Preparation keeps you out of reactive mode. You never want to be in a reactive position, even when you are reacting. If you are not thinking ahead of the other side, then they are thinking ahead of you. When they get ahead of you, you move into reactive mode and they take control of the negotiation.

Nothing is more important than being prepared. When you are fully prepared, negotiation is just a matter of executing your plan. If you understand your opponent's motivations, your plan should lead you to a great result. This is easier said than done. To be fully prepared you must also have considered the following tasks.

BATNA: The Best Alternative to a Negotiated Agreement

A fundamental negotiation concept is BATNA. This means understanding what will happen to you and your opponent if no agreement is reached. Much leverage is gained by simply knowing your opponent's BATNA and by being honest with yourself about your own BATNA from the very beginning. To understand your opponent's BATNA, you need to understand their motivation. Motivation is discussed in depth in chapter 6. You can understand BATNA by answering three questions. (1) What will happen to your opponent's client or company if no agreement is reached? (2) What will happen to your opponent (individually) if no agreement is reached? (3) Do you have competition for this agreement?

Three Questions to Determine an Opponent's BATNA

1. What will happen to your opponent's client or company if an agreement is not reached?
2. What will happen to your opponent (individually) if an agreement is not reached?
3. Do you have competition for this agreement?

Three Question to Determine Your BATNA

1. What will happen to your company or client if you don't reach an agreement?
2. What will happen to yourself if you don't reach an agreement?
3. Can you find a replacement for that which you're negotiating?

The people you negotiate against are usually not representing themselves. The negotiator may be a lawyer or a salesperson or buyer. In each such event, they are acting as an agent for their client or company. So, the first question to consider is, "What will happen to the opponent's company or client if an agreement is not reached?" For example, will the company lose an opportunity? Will they go out of business? Say you are looking to buy a car. If you don't buy the car, will the company suffer? Will the client sue or be sued? Explore all of the other side's potential alternatives.

The second question is, "What will happen to the individual if an agreement is not reached?" The answer to this question gives insight into the personal motivation of the negotiator. As discussed later, in more detail, the individual's motivation is one of the driving forces in any negotiation. Think about the individual. Is it a lawyer who is afraid to try a case? Is it a seller who needs to make quota? Is the person having a good year or a bad year? What motivational level is the person operating on? The explanation and understanding of the individual will pay off throughout the negotiation.

The third question is, "Is there competition for this agreement?" Often, my opponent's BATNA becomes obvious when this question is answered. If I were trying to sell Coca Cola as the exclusive cola for a concert hall, I would be keenly aware of Pepsi's position in this market because if my product is easily replaceable by a comparable product my opponent has a good BATNA. I must be aware of such alternative positions during the negotiation. On the other hand, if I have no competition then I can be more aggressive.

The principle of supply and demand operates when evaluating BATNA. Think about a free-agent contract. If the athlete is the only all-star, left-handed pitcher on the free-agent market, he will demand a high price. Several teams need strong left-hand pitching, and they will all be interested in this player. A team's BATNA may be settling for a lesser left-handed pitcher or signing none at all. These alternatives are less satisfactory than signing the all-star pitcher. On the other hand, if there are three left-handed, all-star pitchers on the free-agent market in the same year, the teams will have more options. The alternative—getting a different all-star to fill their need—is not a bad BATNA.

This next example reminds us that BATNA shifts as the surrounding conditions shift. If three all-star first basemen are available, the teams may feel secure in offering less of a premium for any of the three. However, after the first one is signed, the supply of all-star first basemen diminishes. After the second one is signed, we are back to the earlier example with the left-handed starting pitcher. The third player may be able to demand a premium price, because the remaining teams without an all-star first basement do not have a satis-factory BATNA.

Now think about how BATNA changes when there are three all-star first basemen but only two teams that need—and can afford to pay premium price for—a first basemen. It seems the first basemen will be scrambling to sign first, because the remaining two are going to be bidding down each other's price.

To understand your own BATNA, you must ask yourself the same three questions. In doing this, it is very important to be honest with yourself about the available alternatives. If you are not honest with yourself at the beginning, you will pay for it in the end. For example, if you are in a lawsuit and you think you have a great claim, you will be very aggressive. This will cause you to overvalue your case, and you may leave a good offer on the table.

> Honesty with yourself is critical when evaluating your BATNA.

The first question you have to ask yourself is: "What will happen to my company or client if an agreement is not reached?" Just like you did with your opponent, explore your own alternatives. Will you be stuck in a lawsuit? Will your company miss an opportunity? Will your manufacturing plant produce at less than full capacity? Examine your company or client needs and their potential responses if an agreement is not reached. Do research on your own client.

You also need to ask what will happen to yourself. As discussed later, it's important to understand your own motivation. Why are you doing this deal? Are you buying the car because you like it? Are you buying the car because you need it? Are you trying to do a good job for your client? Will your client fire you if you don't reach an agreement?

Finally, you need to ask yourself if you can find a replacement for that which you're negotiating. Do you have to have the Chevy or can you go down the street and buy a different model? Will another bank give you better loan terms? For example, if you are unemployed and searching for work, negotiating a salary is difficult because your BATNA is more job searching. On the other hand, if you have a job that you like and are being recruited away from that firm, negotiation is easier because your BATNA is to continue at a job you like.

A great example of understanding BATNA comes from the clinic/HMO model discussed earlier (in the questioning chapter). In that case, the HMOs felt in control because they believed they were difficult to replace. They typically controlled 25 percent of my client's revenue and concluded that our BATNA was to replace it with other HMOs. Their position changed when they understood our true BATNA. . . .

In each case, we were the dominant provider of a particular specialty, so our BATNA was to service the same patients as out-of-network providers. Out-of-network providers can charge more than in-network providers because they don't have the security of the steady business an HMO network brings them. However, our clinics enjoyed security of steady business without the help of the HMO because we were the only specialist in the market. Therefore, our BATNA may have led to making more money (with more administrative headaches) than the HMO would provide. In addition, the HMO's BATNA was to try to convince patients to be insured by them, even though they didn't provide in-network coverage to the dominant specialists in town. In each case, we were able to convince the HMOs to provide higher reimbursements for our providers. Shifting their perception of our BATNA was critical to this success.

Elements of The Strategic Plan

Map Out the Deal Maze

A business deal is like a maze. The standard maze on paper is a child's game. Like a bird, you see the maze from a removed perspective. Most mazes are easily solved on paper—to do so, you need only vision and planning. You can see the problem before you, so vision is not an issue. Your planning involves looking ahead at your options and choosing the best ones.

When you are actually inside the high walls of a physical maze (like a rat), the challenge is greater. You can't see around the next corner. Your sense of direction becomes confused. Different sections start to look the same. You cannot see the big picture. Finally, you just hope to get to the end any way that you can. To succeed, you need to employ vision and planning—but also memory, insight, and anticipation. Memory, insight, and anticipation are all imperfect tools. We rely on them, but they are not completely reliable. When you are in the maze, even your vision is limited. It is far better to consider your options before you enter the maze than it is to figure it out as you go.

If you have a plan and a map in advance, getting through the maze is much easier. You plan the most efficient route. You recognize certain landmarks. You maintain your sense of direction. You get through the maze on your own terms.

Preparation of a strategic plan vastly improves your chances for success in the deal maze. If you know what you want to achieve and the route you want to take to get there, you will make better deals. You will be able to see around the next corner. You will not make important decisions on the spot. You will know when a deal is such that it is better to just walk away.

Prepare Budgets for Both Time and Expense

You never have unlimited time or money for a transaction. Preparation helps control your budgets. You need to know how much time and money you have for the negotiation, and you should also have an idea of the time and money your opponent plans to spend. If you don't know what you can tolerate for this deal, then you will be surprised at some point deep into negotiation. These are those moments when you realize, "This is taking too long," or decide, "Let's just get this deal done." These thoughts are not symptomatic of impatience; they are indicators of a failure to properly budget the time or money actually needed to complete the negotiation.

Your budgets for time and money spent on the negotiation are material factors in determining the outcome of a negotiation. Time and money spent in preparation saves many multiples later on. For example, with proper preparation, you will create the right team up front. If you haven't done so and then you have to bring in somebody later for a particular issue, someone will have to spend time educating the new member as to the status of the negotiation. If your time budget is low, then the quality of the new person's contribution will suffer because they are not fully educated.

Your opponent also has time and money constraints. If you understand these, you can use them to your advantage. If you know that a home has been on the market for a long time (e.g., the house is empty, so the family is likely paying two mortgages and may, therefore, have a strained financial budget), you can probably make a lower offer than the asking price. If you buy a car at the end of the month, you might gain an advantage over a seller who needs to sell the car to make the end-of-month quota. These are both examples of sellers who are at the end of their time budget.

Gain Perspective From 40,000 Feet

A bird's-eye view is a great perspective to see from. Birds are above the fray. They see a situation from outside of the situation. Proper planning allows you to see the deal from outside of the deal. You can think through various scenarios, test dead ends, and create alternative responses. Preparation gives you a better perspective from which to make your decisions.

We have all watched football games on television. We see the open receiver that the quarterback did not see. We see the opening on the left when the running back cuts to the right. Why do we see these things that professional athletes don't? Do we have better vision than they do? No. Do we understand the game better than they do? No. But we do have the advantage of perspective. We can see much more of the field because our view is from a better perspective, high above the field.

The quarterback is on ground level, trying to see the field over and around huge defensive linemen. That's hard enough, but it gets harder. Every play, the quarterback goes through a dance few will ever experience. In sixty seconds, he is thrown to the turf and two defensive linemen, each weighing over 300 pounds, land on him. Then he gets up, goes back to the huddle, and receives the play. He chooses the formation and snap count, and then calls the play in the huddle. Moving up to the line, he observes the defensive formation, checks his play against that formation, and calls an audible when he notices the left linebacker threatening a blitz. He reviews in his mind the location of each of his five receivers. He calls the snap count, takes the ball, and moves seven steps backward.

He spots the receiver open short and left, throws the ball, and then is thrown to the turf and pounced on by another defensive lineman.

It is a small wonder that even NFL quarterbacks make mistakes. Their job is impossible without thorough preparation. Although their job seems complicated, it's no more difficult (mentally) than a complex business deal.

Now, imagine you are at the negotiating table. You have in front of you a forty-page contract. Your opponent has just offered to buy 10,000 widgets at full price, but only if you can deliver them all within ninety days. You want to accept the concession and move on, but it's not so simple. How does the new term affect your cost? Will it change the insurance provisions? Can you produce on time, given the seasonal weather at your company's factory in Asia? How much production capacity do you have left at the factory? What happens if you make the agreement and then fail to deliver? All of these questions must be answered before you can respond. This is the moment of truth.

Think about two different potential responses.

Seller No. 1, Bob, did not prepare enough to understand his opponent's motivation. He didn't know that his buyer would be looking for the security of having all his widgets delivered in time to manufacture his products for Christmas. Bob didn't prepare in advance for the possibility of his buyer's need for a rush order, so he didn't know the answers to the questions running through his client's head. His response: "We will do everything we can. Let me confirm our short-term capacity and get back to you." His buyer's response: "Great, call me when you know more." Bob went home without the order.

Seller No. 2, Murray, understood his buyer's motivation. He prepared in advance for the possibility of a rush order. He researched potential questions. He knew he could deliver up to 25,000 widgets within sixty days. He knew the answers to other critical questions. Murray's response: "Absolutely. If you can get me the P.O. right now, we will have no problem filling the order." Murray's buyer then gave him the P.O. and Murray went home with a fat commission.

That is the difference proper preparation makes.

> *"Call me when you know more . . ."*
>
> *or . . .*
>
> *"Thanks for the order."*
>
> *That is the difference proper preparation makes.*

Use Preparation to Intimidate

Preparation can be intimidating. Proper preparation enables you to take a strong position in those places where being less prepared may leave you uncertain. If you fully understand the transaction and research it thoroughly, you will encounter questions that are very likely to come up long before the negotiation. When you know these questions, you can analyze them, look at various alternatives, and arrive at the answer that is most advantageous to you. When the question comes in the negotiation, you will then answer it with certainty and with clarity. You can do this because you know that the answer you are giving is correct. If you are not certain of the answer, know that certainty is difficult to fake—and faking it can burn you later.

I was once in mediation over a construction project. Our client was a subcontractor who had worked on the project but had received only partial payment. The work had been performed over two years, and the main issue was whether the unpaid work was performed directly for the individual property owner or for the owner's company, which had been formed when the project was partially completed, but had become insolvent shortly thereafter. The owner had directly requested the work of the subcontractor, but the subcontractor had sent some of the bills to the company. There was no written contract.

In preparing for the mediation, I reviewed a costly, un-related order from earlier in the case. This issue had arisen in an unrelated discussion earlier. It stated that the project was a single project and could not be divided into two phases. We researched the law on this part, and found it favorable to our client. At a critical juncture of the mediation, the mediator pointed to a body of law dealing with the owner's liability on a multiphase project. Because of our preparation, I was able to immediately respond, saying that the judge had already eliminated that defense and showed him the order. The mediator agreed. We eventually settled the case, with our client receiving about 25 percent higher than we expected. I believe the quick response to that question put money in our client's pocket.

> *Knowing the details is invaluable. Being able to defuse your opponent's argument quickly is good for your position—and can make your opponent hesitate before taking another aggressive position.*

A great lawyer I worked for, Hank, was a master of the tactic I call, "Doesn't everybody know that?" As the young associate, I had been more familiar than Hank with the specific details or case law of his complex lawsuits. I typically briefed Hank before the negotiations began. I pointed out case law and testimony that helped us. If he didn't remember the testimony, I brought him the transcript and showed it to him. He might be surprised, but he just took it all in. Then, thirty minutes later, Hank talked to the other lawyer as if he (Hank) had been focused on this key testimony. He acted surprised that the other lawyer was even challenging it. More than once, I heard Hank quote case law to another lawyer, saying something like, "That's the <u>Smith</u> case exactly. There is no argument against it." He was referring to the case as if it was common knowledge when, in fact, he had learned of it just minutes before the meeting.

This type of preparation can quickly move your opponent's motivation where you want it. As in the case example above, the opposing lawyer, "Bob," felt unprepared and, perhaps, believed Hank was smarter than him. This led him to make concessions to get the deal done just to avoid a disastrous result.

Question and Listen to Get the Answers You Want

Full preparation includes preparing to ask questions and preparing to listen. The purpose of questioning your opponent is to extend your preparation by gaining a complete understanding of your opponent and obtaining early commitments. The questions you want to ask and the commitments you need are determined during your preparation phase. When you are fully prepared, you are able to run through a series of questions that sound like normal conversation, but are actually scripted. You should know the answers to most of your questions before you go into the negotiation.

As part of my preparation for early negotiation sessions, I prepare a list of answers that I want to get. To emphasize—I do not make a list of questions, I make a list of answers that I want. For example, part of a recent list read:

- He graduated from the University of Minnesota in 1987
- He is a big hockey fan
- Business is strong
- His business is pretty much recession-proof
- He is happy with the work provided so far by my client, except for his specific complaint

Of course, I knew these answers ahead of time. By establishing that he is an '87 University of Minnesota graduate and a hockey fan, I could make a connection because I was at the University at the same time and I am a hockey fan. The other three answers, if I get them, are all commitments on his part. By giving me those answers, he is giving up some arguments he might make much later as we approach the endgame.

The key to effective listening is to focus on the answers to your questions. To do this, you need to know the range of possible answers before you ask the question. This means you need to know the range of answers before you go into the meeting. This is full preparation.

As discussed earlier, when in the questioning phase with an HMO, I ask, "Do you have the authority to make a deal with us that is outside of your normal parameters?" The range of possible answers is yes and no. But it's likely that my counterpart will not simply say yes or no. It is necessary to filter the answer into the "yes" box or the "no" box. As the opponent rambles on about "process" or how "everyone gets the same treatment" or whatever, I can check off the right box and then move on to the next question. Usually, follow-up questions are necessary, such as, "Do you mean to say . . . ?" It's also effective to say, "Is it your position that . . . ?"

Before starting, you need to decide which type of questions you want to ask (see chapter 2). This depends on your purpose. Do you know what you expect your opponent to say? Are you truly gathering information? Prepare to ask questions with a finite range of answers. "What color was the traffic light?" can only be answered as red, green, or yellow. "What color was his shirt?" can be answered as green—forest, dark, light, sea foam, bright—or blue, but made out of recycled cotton. If you just need to know if the shirt was green, instead ask, "Was he wearing a green shirt?"

Planning your questions in advance enables you to create your strategy sequence. Most answers are predictable. If you predict the answers with a reasonable degree of certainty, even if it is down to two or three potential answers, then you create your strategy. By understanding how you want to ask each question, you can take the discussion where you want it to go and you can take the deal where you want it to be.

Choose the Right Team

The right team is also essential for negotiations. Bring the best team you can, within your time and money budgets. Look at the eight BIG FORCE skills. Your ideal negotiating team has somebody who is an expert at each skill. However, realistic budgets don't allow for such expertise in most deals. Therefore, you must know your own skill set. You can fill in your weaknesses with other people. And, if you fully understand your opponent, you may be able to let a particular area of expertise go lacking on your team. But be careful. Holes tend to be exposed.

It is conventional wisdom in the negotiation world that you should always negotiate with at least two people on your side. I agree. If you are negotiating by yourself, you can easily become overwhelmed, especially if the other side has two or three people at the table. If your side has at least two people at the table, it seems to make little difference whether the other side has you outnumbered. The big problem occurs when you try to do it alone.

If nothing else, bring along somebody intelligent who can take notes for you. In any case, you should consider assigning the note taking to someone on your team, instead of doing it yourself. Taking notes requires you to divide your attention between what your opponent is saying and what you are writing. If someone else is taking notes, you can concentrate completely on the other side. This will enable you to pick up nuances and body language, which will benefit you in the transaction.

Set Goals

There is much discussion about the impact of setting goals prior to negotiations. I have clients who believe that you get the best results by determining your optimal reasonable result, then stretching that position to start at a point that is unreasonable. This is called the "big pot" position. Others believe that starting at a reasonable position yields better results.

Studies on this issue are mixed, but there is general consensus that negotiators who set goals that are very specific and also difficult to achieve tend to get better results than those with only general goals or no goals at all. If your goal is to sell your house for at least $500,000 and my goal is to buy it for the best price I can get, the contract price will probably be at least $500,000. On the other hand, if my goal is to sell the same house for as much as I can, and your goal is to buy it for less than $500,000, the contract price will probably be less than $500,000.

There is a general consensus that negotiators who start with big pot tactics tend to get better deals than others, but also reach agreement less often. If you are okay with getting no deal, then there is little risk in taking big pot positions. If you need to get a deal done or you want to maintain a relationship, big pot may not be the best tactic.

When setting your goals, it is important to analyze the motivation level of the other side. If your counterpart operates on motivational Level II (safety) and must have a deal, then you might do better by setting aggressive goals. If your counterpart is operating on Level IV (status), then he is more likely to walk away than take a lesser deal. If you really want to reach an agreement, then set reasonable goals. The most obvious contradiction to this principle is when someone absolutely needs the deal, because the other side can drive a hard bargain. Think about a recently engaged couple shopping for the right engagement ring and the bride "just has to have the big stone." If the seller is a good negotiator, that groom is going to pay full price for the ring.

Here is how it works: A couple walks into a jewelry store and the seller greets them. The seller's initial goal, knowing nothing about the couple, is to gather information about them. He uses this information to set his goal for the transaction. Through questioning, he determines that the couple recently became engaged and they have come to the store together to pick out the engagement ring. He also determines that the couple is well dressed and that, though dressed casually, the bride-to-be is wearing a fairly expensive necklace. He concludes that the new bride-to-be wants a large, expensive engagement ring and that she seems to be driving the choice. The groom-to-be does not want to disappoint his new fiancé. Through direct questioning and observation, he concludes that the young couple can afford the expensive ring.

Using all of this information, the seller sets a goal for the negotiation: to sell them one of the largest engagement diamonds he has available. Setting this goal, he begins showing the couple engagement rings from the most expensive box, instead of one of the lower-tier boxes. If he had observed things differently, perhaps hearing the happy couple expressing concern about prices, he would have set his goal differently and shown them rings from a different box. This said, he could have set his goal too high and shown the couple a ring they couldn't afford. In such a case, he likely would have had no sale.

This is how setting goals works. You first need to examine your own needs from a transaction. For example, as you negotiate a salary for a new job, the goal you set if you are just happy to get the job will differ dramatically from the goal you set if you already have a job and are looking for something better. Your own needs should be assessed in terms of a range between the number at which you will walk away from any deal (your "minimally acceptable position") and the best you could reasonably hope to come away with (your "maximum reasonable outcome"). This is the range in which you can expect to reach an agreement, if agreement is possible.

Next, you need to assess your opponent's position. By examining their side of the transaction, you try to establish what, for them, might be a minimally acceptable position and a maximum reasonable outcome.

With this information at hand, you need to decide, strategically, how you want the negotiation to proceed. Are you better off taking a big pot position and negotiating down? Or, should you take a more reasonable position? Remember, an aggressive position at the beginning is less likely to lead to an agreement but it is also likely to give you a better position if an agreement is reached.

Imagine your sixteen-year-old wants to keep the car out until 1:00 a.m. on a Friday night. You have set a negotiation goal to have the car returned by midnight. You have the leverage of being the parent—it is your car, after all. However, you would also like to negotiate an agreement to avoid *ordering* a midnight curfew (and then dealing with the inevitable argument to follow). Your BATNA is that your teenager doesn't get the car but is very angry with you. Your teenager's BATNA is that they don't get the car. In this case, it probably doesn't make sense to start with a big pot position. A big pot position here would be telling your teenager that you want them to come in at 10:00 p.m. The problem with a big pot position in this situation is that you will never hold firm at 10:00 p.m. It is such an unreasonable position that it will never be acceptable to your teenager. It is probably better to take a more reasonable position, perhaps 11:00 p.m., and concede to midnight.

The lesson in this example is that big pot tactics are usually the wrong move if you have hopes for a continuing relationship. If you negotiate regularly by conceding from big pot to more reasonable positions you will lose credibility. Teenager or repeat customer, it is usually a better idea to avoid big pot positions.

SKILL #4
Financial Analysis

Some people make millions of dollars because they understand finances and money. These people can make a balance sheet sing. I knew an accountant who could look at a balance sheet and tell you where the owner buys his suits. (Literally—I saw him do this more than once.) If you have one of those guys working for you, that's great. Work with them and you will have a huge advantage at the negotiation table.

At a minimum, you must be able to understand a balance sheet and income statement. You need to be able to read and manipulate a spreadsheet. Most importantly, you must understand the finances of the deal in front of you and the impact of all potential offers and counteroffers on the deal.

Bottom line: To optimize results, every team needs to have one person who is responsible for and adept at financial analysis. In this context, financial analysis includes the full financial impact of the transaction, both short term and long term. That person needs to be able to analyze the offers of both sides (and, remember, your offers should be analyzed before being made).

Some Basic Definitions.

It is important to have a working understanding of the vocabulary of finance. Misuse of terms can lead to confusion. In the extreme case, it can lead to people thinking the other person is not honest with them when in reality one just didn't understand the fundamental vocabulary of financial analysis. Here are a few definitions that will be useful.

Amortization	Amortization means paying off of debt and also means reduction in value of capital assets over time. This is used to deduct capital expenses of intangible assets over a period of time. In this context, amortization does the same thing with respect to intangible assets that depreciation does for tangible assets.
Appraisal	An appraisal is a professional opinion about the value of an asset. An appraisal differs from a valuation because an appraisal is generally intended to be a neutral opinion of value. A valuation often contains subjective components that make the valuation unique to a particular purchaser as opposed to stating fair market value.
Asset Sale	An asset sale is the sale of all or nearly all of a business' assets. It is a way of transferring the assets of a business to a new company without taking on the liabilities of a stock sale. Asset sales have significantly different tax impact than stock sales.
Balance Sheet	A Balance Sheet is a snapshot of what the business owns at a given moment. It shows the assets of the business and the liabilities of the business as well as the shareholder's equity.
Book Value	This is the value at which the asset is carried on the Balance Sheet. This is typically different than its actual value. Theoretically, the Book Value of an asset can be far different than the actual value in case of an asset which increases in value as it is being depreciated.

Bottom Line	This is the bottom line of a Balance Sheet or Income Statement. The Bottom Line demonstrates the performance after all revenue and expenses are considered.
Due Diligence	Due diligence is the investigation performed by a buyer before a transaction takes place. Due diligence helps a buyer ensure himself that he is getting what he is paying for.
COGS	This means Cost Of Goods Sold. These are the direct costs attached to manufacturing, or acquiring the goods that have been sold. It does not include any overhead, taxes or other costs of operating a business that are not directly related to acquiring or manufacturing the goods sold. You can calculate the COGS by starting with the beginning inventory, adding the cost of goods purchased during the reporting period and subtracting the final inventory.
Depre-ciation	Depreciation has two meanings. On a financial statement it is a method of allocating the cost of an asset over its useful life. In this context, if you buy an asset for cash that will last 30 years, you cannot take the entire expenses in a single year. You must depreciate the asset in accordance with IRS rules. The second definition of Depreciation is the decrease in the assets' value over time. This could be caused by the fact that it is worth less as it goes through its useful life (like a car) or that unfavorable market conditions caused the value of the assets to decrease.
Earnings	Earnings refer to the final profit of a company, at the end of a particular period after all expenses are included. This is the amount of money a business makes in its operation.

EBITDA	This stands for Earnings Before Interest Taxes Depreciation and Amortization. In other words, EBITDA tells you how much money the business would make if it did not have to pay taxes, borrow money or have the tax benefits of depreciation and amortizing its borrowed capital.
Gross Profit	Gross Profit is the revenue minus the COGS. This is the amount of money the company earns selling its products before the costs of the business operation are included.
Gross Revenue	This usually means all revenue that a company receives, without any deduction for expenses.
Income Statement	An Income Statement shows the financial operation of a company over a period of time. You can get an Income Statement for a week or a month or a year or longer. The Income Statement is the fundamental financial statement used in understanding a company's operation.
Net Revenue	This is the gross revenue minus the COGS.
Overhead	These are expenses related to operation of the business, and usually include rent, salary, interest, taxes, employee benefits, and costs of plant operation. It would include all expenses not included in the COGS.

Owner's Compensation	Owners Compensation is usually used when buying or selling a business that is closely held. An entrepreneur who builds a business by himself (or with a few partners) can take money from the business in multiple ways. They can adjust their salary to be high or low. They can have family expenses (e.g. car or cell phone) paid by the business. When evaluating a closely held business, it is necessary to look at all compensation received by the owner and the after acquisition costs of replacing the owner's services. This result will be plugged into the financial statements of the company to be used in the buyer's valuation.
Revenue	This is the amount of money that comes into a business. Be careful of this term because it is often misunderstood. Rather than use the term revenue, I prefer to use more specific terms including gross revenue and net revenue or to specifically describe what financial components are included within the definition of these revenue figures.
ROI	This is Return On Investment. This is a key metric for investors. A deep-pocket investor, such as an adventure capitalist, will adjust the amount of money that they borrow to maximize ROI.
Sale Lease-back	This is a type of a transaction that is really a financing transaction. For example, a company that owns its own building needs capital. Instead of refinancing the building, they sell the building to a new buyer. They might get $1 Million cash for the building. They don't move the operation; rather, they simply begin leasing from the new owner as a landlord. Thus, they create available cash for whatever use they need in the short-term.

Top Line Number or Top Line Revenue	This is another word for Gross Revenue.
Transaction cost	In analyzing any transaction, it is important to know what the transaction costs are. These are the costs related to professional fees and broker's fees as part of the transaction. Professional fees can be lawyers, accountants, appraisers, environmental experts or any other professional that needs to be hired in order to make sure the transaction is completed. These can easily run into six or seven figures on sizable transactions.
Valuation	Valuation is a process, not always a formal process, by which the value of an asset is determined. An appraisal differs from a valuation because an appraisal is generally intended to be a neutral opinion of value. A valuation often contains subjective components that make the valuation unique to a particular purchaser as opposed stating fair market value.

The Cost of Buying and Selling

Financial analysis includes your costs associated with the transaction. If you are selling widgets, you need to know the production cost per widget at various production levels. Additionally, your time and expense budgets are critical. You need to understand the cost of your lawyers and accountants and all other personnel on your deal team. You need to understand how the various deal terms impact your side of the equation as well as your opponent's side of the equation. For significant transactions, an understanding of the tax implication is critical.

When buying or selling a business, the seller has a tax advantage if it is a stock sale (capital gains have lower tax rates) and the buyer loses the ability to expense the cost of the purchase price moving forward. On the other hand, if the buyer purchases assets, he is in a better tax position. Often business sales include noncompetition or earn-out relationships for which the individual entrepreneur selling the business receives payment over several years. This arrangement can produce an annual expense deduction for the buyer but taxation at higher ordinary income levels for the seller. Understanding tax implications is ordinary knowledge among deal lawyers, but is sometimes overlooked by buyers and sellers.

You don't need a PhD in economics. By this, I mean you do not need to understand the generally accepted accounting principles (GAAP) in order to understand the financial impact of a particular agreement. Some transactions are simpler than others. If you buy a bicycle with cash, you simply need to know whether you can afford the cash price. If you buy a bicycle with a credit card, you need to understand the impact of the interest payments on your future finances. If you borrow money to buy a car, the impact becomes greater.

Lease vs. Purchase

One very common situation to understand is the true financial impact of an agreement when you are deciding whether to buy or lease a car. On its face, leasing seems cheaper than buying. The monthly payment is always less. However, owning a car entails considerably more than the monthly payments. In addition to the cost of ownership, you need to consider the value of the vehicle at the end of the lease period.

In the first three years of ownership of a new car, you will pay the down payment, the monthly payments, the insurance payments, the cost of maintenance repairs, and any taxes or other fees you need to pay to own the car. You also need to consider the residual value of the vehicle that you will either keep or give back, depending on whether you buy or lease the car. This residual value is the difference maker.

The first key to the lease/buy analysis is to understand that leasing is simply a form of financing. The second thing is to understand that you have to give the car back at the end of the lease, but you get to keep the car when a car loan is paid off. Leasing is a way to finance the difference between the price of the car now and the residual value for which you can buy the car at the end of the lease. Both the residual value and the purchase price are negotiable.

For example, if you lease a $30,000 car that has a residual value of $20,000, your lease payment will be the product of financing $10,000 over the term of the lease. However, you can negotiate a lower purchase price and a higher residual to minimize the difference between the two. Also, if you negotiate a $28,000 "lease" (the car's current value) and an $18,000 residual you will still have the same monthly lease payment (on a $10,000 loan) but you will be able to buy the car for $18,000 instead of $20,000 at the end of the lease, having made the exact same payments over the term of the lease.

Business Finance

In the business context, financial analysis is much more complicated. You need to understand the value of a particular deal term for your business and for the other side. You need to understand, for example, whether your company is better off selling a million widgets at a lower price or letting your manufacturing plant sit idle. You need to understand your "true cost" involved in any deal. The true cost of a transaction includes the direct cost of the transaction and ancillary items (for example, the time and energy your employees spend on the deal). Shipping is an obvious example, but holding costs are sometimes hidden. Tax impacts of the transaction must also be factored in.

Every business needs to have the advice of a financial expert. This certainly includes understanding balance sheets and income statements. It also includes an understanding of the financial characteristics of your company. Will you need to hire expert labor in the summer? Will the monsoon in China affect the cost of your manufacturing plant there? Should your sales people be renting cars or taking taxicabs when they are on the road? Does it depend which city they are in? A true financial expert can create your balance sheet and income statement and then give you advice on places where you can improve your bottom line. Such experts (almost always CPAs) can be hired full time, as an employee of your company. However, this option is too expensive for most businesses. Accountants are widely available on a contract basis or an as-needed basis at an hourly rate. Find a smart accountant that you trust and you will have a better understanding of the impact of various business deals.

As a person at the negotiating table, it is important that you have a basic understanding of the financial impact of the business transaction in front of you. You should be an expert on that particular deal. To understand the financial impact of the transaction, you can fully prepare to counter your opponent's position.

For example, let's assume you are selling cheeseburgers to convenience stores. You are in the meeting with your buyer. Before the meeting you determine that you need to get at least $0.54 per cheeseburger or it is not worth doing the deal. After much discussion, you are still asking $0.58 per cheeseburger and the buyer is up to $0.56. At this point, the buyer says very clearly, "This is my final offer—take it or leave it." Because you know the financial impact of the deal, you know that $0.56 is an acceptable price, even if it is not the best one that you can get. So you do the deal at $0.56. If you did not understand the financial analysis, which includes the idle employees at the manufacturing plant, you may have rejected the offer of $0.56, because it was a lower price than you envisioned getting. Understanding the financial impact enables you to know when "low" means "too low" and when it means "high enough to accept."

> Understanding the financial impact enables you to know whether "low" means "too low" or "high enough to accept".

To gain a fundamental understanding of finances, some universities permit professional adults to "audit" classes, even if you are not formally enrolled. This means you sit in the class and learn, but you are not graded nor do you receive credit. There are day-long accounting seminars widely available. This provides a topical understanding of the effect of depreciation and other accounting terms. Auditing a class will give you a better understanding.

Financial analysis is, perhaps, the highest payoff of preparation. Financial analysis is complex and often difficult to fully appreciate in the heat of a negotiating battle. If you do your financial analysis fully before you begin to negotiate, you will be well armed to reach an agreement in your favor.

SKILL #5

Opposition's Motivation

The Parable of Frank and Bill

Frank, an account executive at a printing company, rode the train into work today, daydreaming about the future. He is meeting with his customer, Bill, to sign a $2 million order. Frank has been working with Bill for months, and his patience is about to pay off. This is a big deal for Frank—it will bring him a fat commission and put him in the running for Seller of the Year. He will join his company's Ring of Excellence, reserved for sellers who have signed deals for at least $1 million. As he prepares the documentation for the meeting, Frank contemplates the congratulatory emails he will receive. He might even be promoted to the prestigious Large Accounts Group.

When Frank gets to Bill's office, Bill makes him wait for twenty minutes. Frank feels disrespected, but remains patient. He has already waited months so a few more minutes won't really matter. When Bill finally appears, they go to a conference room. Without offering coffee and appearing very much in a hurry, Bill tells Frank that he is sorry but the price is just too high. Bill tells Frank that he has blown his budget on other components and simply cannot pay the price they had agreed to. No deal is possible at that figure.

Frank's world has just changed. Instead of signing a big deal and becoming Seller of the Year, he now faces the wrath of his team for having wasted several months on a dead-end account. Unwilling to lose the deal (and like all good sellers), Frank asks questions. It turns out that Bill has room in his budget if the price is reduced by 5 percent. Frank must make a decision on the spot. On the one hand, $1.9 million is still a large order. His team will still be happy with it. Frank's commission will be reduced but remain sizeable, and he could still join the Ring of Excellence. On the other hand, losing the order would be disastrous: an angry team, no commission, wasted time, and no client for the future. Frank opts for the easy decision and accepts the 5 percent price cut.

The prequel to that meeting is about Frank's client, Bill, the senior buyer. Earlier that morning, Bill discovered that his project was $50,000 over budget because he made a mistake when adding up the associated costs—a mistake that might cost him his job. Nobody wants a senior buyer who is sloppy with numbers, and this was not Bill's first such mistake. Bill needed to cut his costs quickly and without complication. Bill had grown to understand Frank in the months they had worked together. He knew about the Ring of Excellence and what achieving that status would mean to Frank. Bill also knew how to motivate Frank to cut his price. The result: Bill negotiated $100,000 off of Frank's price, came in under budget, and made Frank feel good at the same time.

This is how motivation-based negotiation works. At the end of the day, Bill was able to satisfy his needs by first threatening Frank's social needs (making him wait) and then satisfying Frank's status needs (the Ring of Excellence). The deal was done and everybody was happy. But Frank could have done better. Not understanding your opponent's motivation can be costly. What did Frank do wrong? How could Frank have leveraged the situation more effectively? More on that later.

Negotiation is All About Personal Motivation

> **First Rule of Negotiation:** The only time a negotiated agreement is made is when each side does what the other side wants them to do.

The first rule of negotiation is this: the only time a negotiated agreement is made is when each side does what the other side wants them to do. This is easy when I want to buy a bucket of widgets at the store and the price posted is $19.99 per bucket. I know that if I give them $19.99, they will give me the widgets. It gets harder when the price of a car is listed at $44,500, but you know they will take less. How much less? How can you motivate them to do what you want, which is give you the car in exchange for a lower price?

The first rule of negotiation also states that you can only reach an agreement by motivating the other side to do what you want them to do. Think of a mugger who negotiates the transfer of his victim's wallet by agreeing not to hurt him. Five minutes earlier, the victim had no desire to give his wallet to a stranger. However, at the moment when he gave his wallet away, it was exactly what he wanted do. The threat to his safety motivated him to give away his wallet.

The mugger knows he is committing a crime and risking jail time or a counterattack. Why would he put his freedom at risk in exchange for forty dollars in the victim's wallet? He is motivated by something else. He might be a drug addict or he might have hungry children to feed. Whatever it is, the reward from the forty dollars motivated him to take a great risk.

Various motivators influence negotiators. To understand negotiation, it is fundamental to understand motivation. You need to know what is motivating the other side. From there, you can develop the strategy and gain the leverage to motivate your counterparts to do what you want them to do.

Maslow's Five Levels of Personal Motivation

Abraham Maslow established a hierarchy of needs. According to Maslow, human beings are motivated by unsatisfied needs, and certain lower needs must be satisfied before higher needs can be satisfied. By way of warning, this book will not give you an academic understanding of Maslow's work. I started with a fair understanding of Maslow's ideas twenty years ago, and developed my system from there. My version of Maslow's theories certainly varies from those who are experts in his theories—but my version works in negotiation.

Understanding how personality affects negotiators provides a great advantage. Some call it empathy, but that is just the beginning. An empathetic negotiator has started to understand his opponent's needs and wants. When you begin to understand your opponent's personality, you can begin to understand the underlying motivations. When you understand those motivations, you can usually figure out a way to drive the bargain to your side of the table. Here are Maslow's five levels of motivation, in descending order:

Maslow's Five Levels of Motivation

	Level V	
Self-actualization	Order, beauty, and knowledge	
	Level IV	
Status	Self-esteem, recognition, and reputation	
	Level III	
Social	Sense of belonging or love	
	Level II	
Safety	Physical security	
	Level I	
Physiological	Food and water	

Lower levels of need must be satisfied before a higher level can be addressed. For example, an individual will risk their safety (Level II) if they need to find food (Level I). Like a pyramid, the steps at the bottom must be solid before the needs at the top can be reached. If safety needs are threatened, they must be adhered to before status needs can be addressed. For example, even a self-actualized, art-loving person will leave a burning building to save his life rather than stay to save the art.

The first four levels are states of deficiency. In these states we sense that something is missing. We feel anxious (scared or lonely or thirsty) if these needs are not met. For example, we feel hungry because we lack food. To satisfy these needs, we take action to fill the missing element. We eat when we are hungry. We seek people when we are lonely. You can motivate people acting on any of the first four levels by providing them the missing element or, more often, by introducing an opportunity for them to fill the need themselves. You can also motivate them by threatening to remove an element. Bill did this to Frank by threatening to remove the big deal that supported his status needs.

Level V—self-actualization—is the growth level. It is made up of two sublevels: cognitive needs (the need to know and understand) and aesthetic needs (the need for beauty). We move through these sublevels toward self-actualization.

Maslow's hierarchy is useful in understanding negotiations because people move up and down within the hierarchy. An individual who has a secure sense of belonging (Level III) in their company may seek to satisfy personal status needs (Level IV). However, if job security is threatened (job loss is a Level II safety concern), that need will require attention first. While movement between levels regularly occurs, traumatic shifts can be unsettling. The parable of Frank and Bill illustrates this important point, as Bill's announcement threatens Frank's big deal.

Reasons versus Motivation

A negotiator's "reason" is the explanation they give to them-selves and their client for why a particular deal is a good one. Sometimes it's just an excuse, but usually the reason is a genuine, logical basis for accepting a deal. For example, a couple selling their house decides to accept an offer for 10 percent less than the asking price because it might be months before they see another offer. Likewise, the plaintiffs' lawyers, discussed above, decided that accepting a small amount was

A Personal Lesson

As a young lawyer, I was eager to take cases to trial. Our firm defended insurance companies on many small personal injury issues. These cases went to young lawyers, like myself, to help give us experience. I worked up all my cases. I wanted to be-come an experienced trial lawyer, so I had to take cases to trial. That was my motivation. To my disappointment, case after case was settled by the insurance companies for small amounts, and usually just before going to trial. While these small settlements are considered victories, I was not gaining trial experience. I expressed my disappointment to a senior lawyer who explained to me that my eagerness to go to trial, even as a young lawyer, was intimidating to some plaintiff lawyers. They assumed I had a great case or was a great trial lawyer (I was not) and so they settled for a small amount rather than risk losing the trial and getting nothing.

Armed with this advice, I thought I understood plaintiff motiva-tion. They did not want to try cases. So I tried a new strategy. Two months before trial, I would send my final and best settle-ment offer to the plaintiff's lawyer, explaining that if the offer was not accepted within ten days, it would be withdrawn and we would go to trial. My strategy backfired. It created the ap-pearance of a young lawyer eager to settle. The plaintiff law-yers sometimes drove harder bargains to test my will. In most cases, the insurance companies still settled just before trial. My strategy failed because my mentor's lesson taught me only to understand my opponent's reason, not the underlying motiva-tion. These are two unique qualifiers in the world of negotiation.

better than working and potentially getting nothing. These are reasons.

A negotiator's "motivation" is something else. The home sellers above were motivated to sell because they could not afford to carry two mortgages and were afraid to risk waiting for another offer that might not come. Their security (Level II) was threatened because failure to sell their home might force them to use all of their savings, which could lead to possible bankruptcy. They were motivated to sell by a need to maintain their security. If they could easily pay the holding costs for both houses, they would not have sold the house at a discount.

Different lawyers might give the same reason for settling ("It was not worth the risk of going to trial"), but have different motivations. The plaintiff's lawyer might be motivated to avoid taking a bad case to trial either to avoid losing the battle (self-esteem, Level IV) or because doing so would keep their clients happy (belonging, Level III). Perhaps some of them need the money (security, Level II).

Motivation is the dog, and reason is the tail of the dog. Reason follows from motivation. Your opponent will not agree with you unless he is motivated to do so and has a reason to do so. That said, if you provide the motivation, your opponent usually provides his own reason.

The purpose of this book is to move you past giving your opponents a reason to come to your side of the table and into the realm of giving them the motivation to give you what you want. If you can control the dog, the tail will follow. If you understand your opponent's motivation, you can use it to move him to your desired result.

The personal nature of negotiations is perhaps the best edge a small David company has when negotiating with a big Goliath company. Regardless of the resources available, the negotiator (or team) on the other side of the table is personally responsible for the results. Like each of us, the negotiator is moving through life balancing needs, wants, and pressure from many sources. If you can get the negotiator's agreement, the rest of the company will fall in line.

> If you provide the motivation, your opponent will provide the reason.

Motivation Level I: Basic Physiological Needs

Physiological needs are basic, human, functional needs—including our need for air, water, food, sleep, and so forth. When these needs are not satisfied, we immediately want to attend to them to alleviate the sickness, irritation, or pain they cause.

A good negotiator never walks into a meeting hungry or thirsty or tired. Getting plenty of sleep and staying in good physical condition will get you better deals. People get tired, hungry, and thirsty in long meetings. In big deals, players move to satisfy these needs. Even a BIG FORCE negotiator will be affected if hungry or tired.

Level I is easy to satisfy. If you are hungry or thirsty or tired, ask for a break or end the meeting. Don't make important decisions when tired. Take a break and sleep on it. Preparation is critical here. Set your goals before entering the tension, emotion, and strain of meetings. This will give you the ability to say no even though your fatigue is telling you just to get the damn thing over with.

On the other hand, if you notice that your opponent is tiring and you feel fine, don't ask for a break. In certain circumstances you may not want to consent to a break. As you get to know your opponents, you may find that they need frequent breaks, drink lots of water, or eat often. Consider whether you want to provide for these needs or force them to ask for a break whenever they want something.

Be aware of how schedules can set you up to be tired, hungry, or jet-lagged. Fly in a day early, if you can. You usually have some influence over the time of a meeting, so set it when you will be fresh. Sometimes, the attack on your Level I need is not as obvious as simply setting a meeting time. Anyone who has mediated a business dispute knows this is true.

Years ago, I was part of a legal team defending a school district that had been sued by a student. The student claimed she was blinded in a school accident. Any settlement up to $100,000 (the insurance policy limit) was to be paid by the school's insurance company; and the school district had to pay any award greater than that. As the case approached trial, we had several strong defenses to the claim (including that no doctor could confirm the student was actually blind). The plaintiff's lawyer was seeking a $7 million settlement. The insurance company offered only $8,000. The school district (our client) wanted the insurance company to offer more money, because losing the trial meant the jury had decided the girl was blind—and this would cost the school district big damages.

We entered mediation to try to negotiate a resolution. Mediation started Thursday at 5:00 p.m. and continued past midnight with little progress. The mediator broke off the meeting then, stating that it would continue at 5 p.m. on Friday. In addition, he ordered the parties to appear in court Friday morning at 8:30 a.m. to argue a legal issue that had come up in negotiations. Everyone went to bed late, and then got up early for court. Then it was back to our offices to prepare for the evening's mediation session.

The mediator's real reason for the early court hearing was to deprive the parties of sleep. A senior lawyer on our team knew this. He told us to go home after the hearing and sleep for two hours, which we did. We returned well ahead of the 5 p.m. mediation start time. The case was finally settled after midnight. The insurance company paid more than ten times their original offer and the plaintiff accepted less than 5 percent of his original demand. Our client got the result they wanted, a settlement under $100,000. I believe our success in achieving a settlement on that Friday was largely because our team members were less exhausted than the rest of the players.

While you won't negotiate deals with people who are actually starving, the people on the other side of the table are often hungry or thirsty. Be aware of their condition, as well as your own. Like young David in the Bible, individuals and small companies must take steps to protect against attacks on their Level I needs. This can be a danger area because David is without the resources of Goliath. In addition, Goliath is often hosting the meeting and will try to control the refreshments and the agenda. Some protective measures are obvious:

- Get a good night's rest.
- Eat a good meal before the session.
- Don't come in hung over.
- Carry cereal bars in your briefcase (in case you need a snack).

These fundamental preparations should be second nature to you for any meeting expected to last more than three hours.

Other protections are based on your lifestyle. Don't smoke. Many business people see a tobacco addiction as a character flaw. Most offices in North America no longer allow you to smoke indoors, so you will have to ask for a break to go outside. As a long meeting progresses, everyone (including you) will get tired of taking breaks for you to smoke. You will stop asking for breaks and will get agitated by your cravings just when the meeting is getting to crucial stages. Smokers have a huge disadvantage in long negotiating sessions. Besides, smoking is bad for you. Quit.

Be in good physical condition. Eating well and exercising regularly gives you energy every day. As a long meeting gets longer, your body and brain will have more stamina than those on the other side. If your brain keeps getting its full blood supply and your opponents' brains don't, you have an advantage.

Before the meeting, you need to protect the schedule and agenda. If you're in a hotel, you can manipulate the scheduled start time of the meeting to be either early or late, whichever you prefer. The other side gets to sleep in their own beds, but this can be a disadvantage—it comes with the distractions of kids, spouses, and regular habits. You are in a hotel, free of such distractions. If you set a meeting time for 10 a.m., you can accomplish several things. You can wake up, work out, eat a late breakfast, and prepare for the meeting without distraction and arrive refreshed and ready. The other side will go through their morning routine: arrive at the office at 8 a.m. and then fidget around while waiting for the meeting to start by returning their phone calls and email. They may even get distracted with another project. By 1:00 p.m., they will be hungry and want a break, but you won't need lunch yet. You'll have an advantage during that time.

During the meeting, drink plenty of water. If you usually drink coffee or soda during the day, you should drink the same thing during the meeting. But add some water along the way. You will feel better. Make sure to ask for a break when you need one—whether to use the bathroom, wash your face, or just walk around the block. Be careful not to abuse this or you may find yourself out of "time-outs" later in the meeting. If meetings go longer than four hours and you are hungry, insist on a meal break or order food in.

Schedule your flight home as late as possible. You can always use stand-by on an earlier flight if the meeting ends sooner. A later flight avoids the possibility of concessions so you can rush to make your plane's departure time. Flying out the day after the meeting reverses the time pressures. You can stay all night, but the other side needs to get home to dinner or to their kid's hockey game. Such reversals are effective, but may cost you extra time and money. Consider making room in your time and money budgets.

You can take advantage if the other side fails to protect themselves. If the other party is a smoker who needs regular breaks, you can time discussion of an important issue to happen at a point just before reasonable break times, but late enough so the cravings settle in. If the opponents look tired and you are fresh, don't take a break until they ask for one. Consider making the meeting last longer, if they are tired—or shorter, if you are tired.

When you are the home team, the situation is reversed. If the other side has a flight pressure, you can use this to your advantage. Time an important point to rush your opponents to a concession. Schedule the meeting so that you can stick to your regular routine. Order food in (or not) to your best advantage.

As you can see, you can protect or attack opponents operating on Level I just by planning ahead. The key is just to understand that Level I needs are absolutely critical and will not go away unless attended to. By planning ahead, you can minimize the adverse effects of your own Level I needs.

Motivation Level II: Safety Needs—The Comfort Zone

Level II is the comfort zone. When you are out of your comfort zone you are feeling threatened on this level. Safety needs involve establishing stability and consistency, including physical safety. But these needs are mostly psychological. In the modern world, a businessperson is more likely to have market share attacked than they are to be eaten by a wild animal. Satisfying Level II needs means feeling comfortable and secure in your job, your family, and your surroundings.

The best way to threaten your opponent's Level II needs is to actually be smarter and more prepared than they are. There's no shortcut to this. If you are completely prepared you are confident, knowledgeable, and in control of the meeting. At some point in the meeting, your opponents will realize that you are ahead of them. They will feel their security threatened. In most cases, their behavior will be predictable, based on your preparation. When this happens, you have gained the advantage. Press your advantage and close the deal.

The better you know your opponents, the better you can understand them in relation to Level II needs. Listen to how they talk about their spouse, their job, or their boss. There is a great difference between someone who smiles when a family member calls their cell phone and someone who rolls their eyes. Listen to how they talk about their children. Is your opponent secure in the job? Is the marriage stable? Does the opponent truly understand the deal (or try to bluff through it)? All of these are Level II matters that can be exploited during the negotiations.

All this personal pressure tugs at your opponent and serves as a distraction to them. These pressures also drive decision making. Negotiators whose safety is threatened will move swiftly to protect that interest.

> If you control the matches and gasoline, it's easy to sell fire insurance.

In real-life negotiations, safety concerns rarely relate to actual physical safety. Rather, "danger" means the potential loss of something important. Potential job loss is a safety issue. Less dramatic but more common is the safety of a negotiator's relationship with the boss. Even loss of a single job commission can create a safety concern.

Secrets create safety concerns. Some people's secrets are so debilitating that they fear (rightly or wrongly) that revealing them would turn their world upside down. Secrets that people act to hide include problems like alcoholism, gambling, cheating on a spouse, stealing, or fear of discovery of some other bad act. Perhaps the most common secret people want to conceal is that they have made a mistake.

When people make a mistake, often their first instinct is to cover it up and hope the mistake cures itself. Sometimes it does. But sometimes people compound their mistake by covering it up. If you can offer a way to permanently bury a prior mistake, you will satisfy your counterpart's need for safety. In doing so, you can get something of greater value in exchange.

Now, let's go back to Bill and Frank. Bill masked his budgetary mistake (to his own boss) by taking some skin out of Frank's sale. If Frank had known about Bill's mistake, he could have used Bill's motivation to earn himself an even bigger commission. Frank could have said, "I know you have budget issues, but I have to hold my price. However, if we make this a two-year deal, we can push the $100,000 into next year." If Frank had done that, he would have buried Bill's mistake (satisfying Bill's Level II issues), and would have signed a big order for next year at the same time.

How could Frank have discovered Bill's mistake? The two men had been working together on the deal for months. If Frank truly understood Bill, Frank might have figured out that Bill can be sloppy. Knowing this, he could have guessed the possibility of such a mistake from Bill's abrupt behavior at the closing meeting. From there, Frank could have tailored questions to determine whether Bill had made a mistake and then he could have proceeded accordingly. At the right time, an honest question like, "Did you make a budget mistake?" would have been very powerful—and ultimately lucrative.

Avoid cover-ups in dealing with your own mistakes. A cover-up creates weakness. Even if your cover-up is successful, you will pay a price for it. You will always fear discovery. This will affect how you deal with certain matters during the negotiation. For example, you'll be less likely to take a strong position in the future for fear it may lead to discovery of your mistake.

When the mistake is discovered (and it almost always is) your cover-up will often cause more pain than the original mistake. (This happened to Presidents Richard Nixon and Bill Clinton.) When your cover-up is blown, you will lose credibility and the trust of your opponent. You will experience Level II insecurity. For the rest of that negotiation, your opponents will be able to exploit this insecurity in two ways: (1) they can come out and say, "I don't believe you" at the right time; thus, the trust in you is lost, making it harder for you to motivate them. On the other hand, admitting your mistake is a strong move. In doing so, you often prevent the other side from exploiting the mistake. Let's take a look at what this looks like in our original example of Bill and Frank. If Bill had admitted he had blown his budget, this would have pinned Frank into a corner. . . .

So, at this point, Frank and Bill both know that Bill is backing out of a verbal commitment, but Frank's options are limited. Frank could either walk away from the deal or renegotiate his price. Bill knows that Frank is more likely to reduce his price than leave the deal on the table.

Bill's admission of mistake to Frank is effective because he does three things: (1) He credibly explains the mistake and how it affects both of them, (2) he apologizes for the mistake and accepts the blame for it, and (3) he puts himself in position to not be able to correct the mistake, unless Frank makes a concession. If you can do all three of these things, you can generally get away with such an admission—once—during a negotiation.

When Bill admits he had made a mistake, he demonstrates that he is so secure that Level II safety is not even a consideration, his Level III need (to be liked by Frank) is so well satisfied that he doesn't care that Frank will be angry at him for changing the price, and his Level IV self-esteem need is so well satisfied that he can give away some of it without threatening his Level IV status.

By being direct with Frank about the mistake, Bill feeds into Frank's Level III need for respect. If Frank is at Level II or III, he will feel that Bill made a concession by giving him this respect. If Frank is also at Level IV, then the admission will feed Frank's self-esteem need. Lack of an explanation shows disrespect, which will irritate Frank if he is trying to fill his own Level IV need for self-esteem.

Bill also helps himself by apologizing for the mistake and accepting blame for it. This feeds Frank's Level IV need for respect and creates room for a concession, if Frank is operating on that level. If Frank is operating on Level II and trying to get to Level III, he will want to help Bill solve his problem. In either case, Bill's budget problem is solved and Frank leaves feeling good about giving away $100,000 in revenue.

Level II players can be approached with a carrot, a stick, or both. Depending on the makeup of the player and the deal, one of these approaches will be more effective than the others. The carrot is a solution to the opponents' safety problem, the stick is a direct threat to them, and the hybrid approach offers a carrot and a stick at the same time. The latter two approaches work best for adversarial relationships, while the carrot approach is best when you want a win-win outcome.

The Carrot Approach

If you are in a long-term relationship with the other side it is usually best to use the carrot approach. This approach requires that you understand the safety concerns troubling your counterpart. You must ask probing questions. Get them to talk about themselves. Such information is useful and helps build the relationship. If your counterpart does not trust you, they will not trust the solution you offer.

It is important to be clear here. You must be authentic and you must earn the trust of your counterpart. The solution you offer must be one that genuinely solves your counterpart's problem. Obviously, you will not offer a solution unless it is a win for you, but it must also be a win for the other Level II player.

Don't rush to offer a solution. Be sure to understand their real problem. Take your time. Often, the stated problem is less than the whole concern. Sometimes it isn't even related to the real problem.

For example, think about Stan. Stan is meeting with Janet, a young buyer for a large retail chain. Stan wants to sell Janet ten containers of widgets for retail sale. Janet tells Stan that she thinks his widgets are great and will fill a gap in their retail stores. However, she only wants to buy five containers. Stan pushes a little for seven containers (without success) then walks away with an order for five containers. Stan is happy. But he actually missed the boat.

Now, think about Dan. He understands that Janet is on Level II because she is new to her job and has not yet established herself with her company, thus any mistake she makes could threaten her job security. Dan understands that Janet wants to dilute her risk by limiting her buy with any single company. So Dan asks a few questions. He finds out that the cost of five containers consumes half of her budget and that she also plans to buy five containers of widgets from the competition. Janet tells Dan that she wants to see how both widgets perform in the same markets before committing more resources to one or the other. This signals to Dan that Janet is afraid of making a mistake, so she is splitting up the buy to avoid a potentially embarrassing outcome.

Having earned Janet's trust, Dan sees a chance to help her avoid a mistake. Dan knows that Janet's company performed extensive market testing on the competing widgets two years earlier. From this, he knows that his widgets do very well in the Midwest, but that the competition does better in the South. The Midwest is 80 percent of the overall market. When Dan determines that Janet is unaware of the testing, he educates her. He shows her the results and explains why they are significant. If he is fully prepared, he has the old research with him. The result: Janet understands the analysis and Dan gets an order for eight containers.

It is critical that Dan's solution be honest. If he misrepresents the earlier research, Janet will never trust him again. He must point out the places where his competitor's product will work better. Dan is free to interpret the data to his advantage, but he should do so knowing that if Janet thinks he isn't trustworthy, he is out the door regardless of his actual level of trustworthiness. Janet's perception is most important.

The first seller, Stan, thought Janet's problem was deciding where to obtain her ten containers of widgets. But Janet's real problem was that she was afraid of making a mistake because of her lack of historical competitive knowledge. The second seller, Dan, recognized Janet's lack of knowledge and identified this as a Level II safety need. Dan sold her an order that was 60 percent higher than Stan's order and closed his competition out of 80 percent of the market. He also earned Janet's trust. These benefits will continue for years to come. By providing Janet the research as a safety net, Dan satisfied Janet's Level II needs and increased his order. This is how the carrot approach works.

The Stick Approach

The stick approach is the opposite of the carrot approach but also works best on Level II, when your counterpart has safety concerns. It is built on fear and the premise is to attack your counterpart in the place where he is most vulnerable. It's like putting a snake in a sleeping bag. The stick approach is more effectively used in adversarial negotiations (like litigation) than in a long-term buyer-seller relationship.

To use the stick approach, you must first understand your counterpart's Level II safety concern. Is he afraid of getting fired? Is he trying to hide a mistake from his boss? Is he having personal economic troubles? Does he hate snakes?

Once you know why he has safety concerns, you can think about using the stick method. The idea is to expose him to his fear: drive up the intensity of his safety concerns and you will maximize your results. This is why it is beneficial to shop for cars at the end of the month. A car salesman who needs to sell three cars on the final weekend of the month will have safety concerns because of the negative consequences of not making his quota and therefore not earning his expected monthly income.

Because the car salesman needs to sell cars to make his quota, he will be willing to give up some price (and some of his commission) to close a deal. To exploit this, you must make a low (but reasonable) offer to buy a car. He will "go see his manager." When he comes back with a counteroffer, you should politely get up, shake his hand, and leave. If you're right and he has safety concerns, he'll call you back and try to talk you into another offer. Don't raise your price. Appear a little impatient. Eventually, he'll go back to his manager to "talk to him for you." When he returns, don't raise your offer. No matter how many times he goes back to his manager do not raise your offer. After the third visit leave, again. If he stops you, scold him. You told him what you are willing to pay. He can either accept it or not. He'll take one more trip to see his manager. During this trip, he really will be advocating for you. If he needs the deal, he'll cut his own commission to make it happen.

You have to become a bit of a bully to effectively use the stick approach. Bullies find their target's weakness and hit it again and again. But be careful—this approach generally leaves bad feelings and scorched relationships. The stick works in most cases where your counterpart has Level II concerns. Find out what keeps your counterpart up at night and use that to create anxiety and get a better deal.

The Hybrid Approach

Using both a carrot and a stick is one of my favorite tactics. The hybrid approach, or the "two futures close," is used as part of the endgame and is great for closing deals. Even when it does not close the deal, it provides valuable information that you can use later to get the deal done.

To use the hybrid approach, you provide the other side with a comparison of two futures: one threatening their safety and another one offering additional safety. Put another way, one future threatens to move them down a level while the other promises to move them up. One future is a stick and the other is a carrot.

Criminal prosecutors use the hybrid approach all of the time when plea-bargaining. They offer two choices: the defendant can either (1) accept the plea bargain and spend three years in prison or (2) take the chances on losing at trial and going to prison for ten to fifteen years. Another example is a defendant that can (1) testify against the crime boss and be forgiven of the crime or (2) be convicted and go to prison for ten years. In the prosecutor's version of the hybrid approach, the defendant is typically presented with a choice between a bad future and a worse future. Criminal defendants have very little leverage.

The hybrid tactic is also useful in closing business negotiations, in a somewhat different way, as the "two futures close." In this case, it's most effective to present the opposition with a choice between a good future and a bad one. A buyer offers the seller a volume buy at a discount or no deal. On one side, the seller can increase revenue and their commission, which is a good future. Their other choice is to go home empty-handed. A seller with safety concerns will almost always take the deal offered.

Here is a good example of the two futures close. Tom wants to sell his business for $5 million. Jon offered $4.5 million, but the two appear to be at an impasse. Jon goes to Tom's office for one last meeting to try to close the gap. He uses the two futures close.

Jon: Tom, we are really close on this deal. What are you going to do with all that money? [He is setting up the carrot.]

Tom: I suppose I'll just pay off my house and squirrel the rest away. It's not really that much money.

Jon: Four and a half million bucks! I know you. You're going to spend half your time playing golf and the other half with your grandchildren. [This is the carrot side of the hybrid approach.]

Tom: You mean five million, I think.

Jon: I can't get to five. The finance cost will kill me. And everybody is predicting the economy is headed south next year. I am young enough to ride out the recession, but not at five million. [Setting up the stick for the older Tom.] Can you come off of the five at all?

Tom: I can, but not too much. The economy will be fine. [Jon correctly reads that Tom is worried about the economy—a safety concern.]

Jon [with the two futures close]: Listen, if the economy grows, the business is worth five million, but if it doesn't the business is worth less than four. If we cut a deal, I take the future risk. If we don't cut a deal, I may be back here in twelve months with a lower offer. No one knows the future. One of us is right and one of us is wrong. I am offering to split the risk at four and a half million and send you to the golf course [good future] or you can spend a few more years in the salt mine battling the recession [bad future]. If you want to take that risk, it's up to you.

The golf course is the carrot. The future lower offer is the stick, so is the "salt mine" comment. The conversation continues, with the result that Jon eventually buys the company for $4.6 million. He showed Tom the golf course and the possibility of the poor house. Tom took the golf course to satisfy his safety concern.

There are ways to defend yourself when your counterpart employs the hybrid approach/two futures close. If Tom is truly optimistic about the near-term future, he will stand firm. He does not have to sell. Even if he is somewhat worried, he can still defend his position.

To defend against the two futures close, you must demonstrate that the projected bad future is not really so bad. If the bad future means litigating for a year, show them how much you enjoy litigation. I once heard a senior lawyer who was threatened with going to trial remind the younger lawyer, "I am paid very well to try cases. That's why my clients hire me. If you don't take my offer, my month-end reports will look very good."

Here is a potential exchange with Tom defending against Jon's attack:

Jon: Tom, we are really close on this deal. What are you going to do with all that money? [He is setting up the carrot.]

Tom: I suppose I'll just pay off my house and squirrel the rest away. It's not really that much money.

Jon: Four and a half million bucks! I know you. You are going to spend half your time playing golf and the other half with your grandchildren. [This is the carrot side of the tactic.]

Tom: You mean five million, I think.

Jon: I can't get to five. The finance cost will kill me. And everybody is predicting the economy is headed south next year. I am young enough to ride out the recession, but not at five million. [Setting up the stick for older Tom]. Can you come off of the five at all?

Tom [defending while ignoring the cost question]: I've been through good times and bad. In hard times we do more maintenance and in good times we sell more new equipment. It all ends up about the same. You should be able to do 50 percent margins on maintenance. We grew right through the last recession at 8 percent per year. At that rate, I might get five and a half million if I wait a year. You can still buy it for five now, but I need your decision.

Tom has made it clear that he understands the future and that he has been there before. He has even played the hybrid approach back by reminding Jon that it may be more expensive later (stick), but he can get a bargain now (carrot).

A second way to defend against the two futures close is to create a third future—a great move if you can pull it off. The move is to counter Tom's two-future scenario by bringing up a third possibility that is outside the framework your opponent has created. Back to Tom and Jon again:

Jon [using the two futures close]: Listen, if the economy grows, the business is worth five million, but if it doesn't, the business is worth less than four. If we cut a deal, I will take on the future risk. If we don't cut a deal, I may be back here in twelve months with a lower offer. No one knows the future. One of us is right and one of us is wrong. I am offering to split the risk at four and a half million and send you to the golf course [good future] or you can spend a few more years in the salt mine battling the recession [bad future]. If you want to take that risk, it's up to you.

Tom: The business is worth five million right now. If we don't cut a deal, I will sell it to Walbux and you can compete with them [third option/stick]. I already have a meeting set with them for next Tuesday. If we have a signed LOI by then, I will call off my Walbux meeting [carrot].

Another way to defend the hybrid approach is to be unreasonable. In this scenario, Tom would just say, "I don't care if I have to hold it for seven more years, I will not sell it for a penny less than five million." (Note that such a statement is unreasonable only if Tom is actually willing to sell for less than $5 million.)

I am not a fan of this approach. It tends to cut off communication. However, it is effective in disarming the hybrid approach. In our example, Jon now must either pay $5 million or walk away. Of course, he could also choose to ignore Tom's statement. But either way, Tom has successfully thwarted Jon's attempt to put him in the hybrid approach box.

Gravity Maneuvers

Another effective tool with Level II players is a gravity maneuver. Gravity is everywhere, affects everything, and will never go away. A gravity maneuver is any move that is essentially irreversible and has a significant impact on the negotiations.

Gravity maneuvers can be used to make the status quo permanent or convince the other side that you are serious about your position. Gravity maneuvers are especially effective if you are having trouble getting the other side to give you their attention. Gravity maneuvers work well against safety concerns because they bring a dispute to a head. Gravity maneuvers often create anxiety for Level II players by forcing them to choose one action or another when they would prefer to do nothing.

My favorite gravity maneuver occurred in a political situation. A multinational corporation wanted to build its American headquarters in a Minneapolis suburb. Significant political controversy surrounded the proposal. Neighbors argued against the permit application for the headquarters, objecting to both the huge size of the proposed complex and increased motor vehicle traffic from company employees. Nevertheless, the permit application moved through the city process and reached a final award. Technically, the company had permission to build its headquarters. However, an appeals process was available to the neighborhood group.

Normally a builder waits until this appeal time has run out before beginning the project, because if the permit is over-turned, any construction must be destroyed. In the case at hand, the company chose not to wait. Instead, they built the foundation and structural framework for each of the four buildings in less than a week. The buildings went up as if by magic. The appeal never took place and the buildings stand today as the company's world headquarters.

By putting up the structures so quickly, the company sent a message to the neighborhood group telling them two things: (1) that the company expected to win because they were risking millions of dollars, and (2) even if the neigh-borhood won the first appeal, the company would continue to appeal until it prevailed because it had already spent millions of dollars on the project. The stakes changed for the corpo-ration from, "This is a good spot for us," to, "This is where we have invested millions of dollars." If the building permit had been reversed, millions of dollars would have been wasted and more money would have been spent to tear down the buildings.

Gravity maneuvers are sometimes confused with fait ac-compli. Both involve one side taking an action that affects the negotiations. The difference is that a gravity maneuver cannot be undone by the parties while a fait accompli is when one side takes unilateral action that impacts the negotiations. Although they are not the same thing, they are members of the same family. A fait accompli can be reversed or ignored.

Gravity maneuvers, once taken, are outside of the parties' control. If you sue somebody before negotiation, the lawsuit can always be dismissed. If you throw the first punch, your opponent can choose to ignore the punch and not fight. With a gravity maneuver, the game changes for all sides. In the company headquarters example, putting up the buildings permanently altered the posture of the political negotiation.

Another example from the 1960's concerns a football player for the Green Bay Packers. In those days very few players had agents. Vince Lombardi, the team's autocratic coach and general manager, was in charge of negotiating players' contracts every year. One year, the team's all-pro center sent an agent to negotiate for him. When the agent arrived at the office, Lombardi asked him to wait in the lobby while he made a phone call. Five minutes later Lombardi invited the agent into his office, advised him that the player had been traded and, thus, was no longer a member of the Green Bay Packers.

This was a gravity maneuver. Lombardi decided his team could live without the center and decided to send the message that agents were not welcome in future negotiations. Other gravity maneuvers include releasing information to the public, firing an employee (or hiring a replacement), or spending money reserved for one purchase order on a different purchase order. Anything that dramatically changes the posture of the parties and is essentially irreversible by the parties is a gravity maneuver. Cutting off negotiations can be a gravity maneuver, but only if done in such a way that the parties cannot restart the negotiation.

Often the threat alone of a gravity maneuver is enough to bring the other side to agreement. Perhaps the ultimate example of this is actually putting a gun to somebody's head. A loaded gun at their temple can motivate most people. Actually pulling the trigger—which kills any chance of a deal (literally)—is a gravity maneuver. The victim will usually give up his wallet in exchange for his safety, so shooting is unnecessary. By threatening with a gravity maneuver, the other side will often be motivated to do what you want.

As discussed above, Level II safety concerns often circulate around a party trying to hide a previous mistake. If you know about the mistake and threaten to reveal it, you can add value to your side of the deal. But if you actually reveal it, that is a gravity maneuver.

Motivation Level III: Love and Belonging Needs

Human beings are social animals. When we have eaten and feel safe (Levels I and II) we start looking for social groups and places to belong. Most of us are "joiners" to one degree or another. People need to belong to groups—social groups, work groups, or teams, etc. Some people need to hear applause when they do something good. Some need the team looking over their shoulder to motivate them to do better.

People operating on Level III range from social climbers trying to get into the right country club to senior citizen volunteers looking for a way to spend their day. Bureaucrats often operate at Level III. They just want to do their job without making waves. They want to belong (Level III) as opposed to standing out as a star (Level IV).

A Level III player wants to sit at the cool kids' table.
A Level IV player wants to be the coolest kid.

Strivers and Stayers

Level III people come in two types: "strivers" and "stayers." Strivers are dissatisfied with their own group and want to belong to a "better" group, while stayers want only to enjoy the continued acceptance of the group they already belong to. Strivers are trying to move up; Stayers are afraid of moving down.

Strivers

Strivers seek to belong to a different group than the one they are currently in. This need is closely related to Level IV (status), but is different. Strivers are not seeking honor among their own peers. Rather, they seek to join a new peer group that they consider a better fit for them. This difference is important to understand. Strivers don't seek to be the richest people at their public golf course (Level IV). Instead, they want to be average members of the wealthy country club. They want to be on the "elite" sales team. They want to be on the sales reward trip to Hawaii. Strivers look for better schools for their kids, better neighborhoods, and better country clubs. Strivers prefer to be average students in an Ivy League school than valedictorian at a lesser university.

Take note that "better" as used here means richer, safer, more popular, more fun, more religious, more successful, or more of whatever is in the eye of the striver. Strivers think, to some degree, in terms of how they are treated, but mostly they just want to be accepted by the "better" group.

Strivers are friendly to change. They present a great opportunity for sellers. Strivers are willing to change loyalties and can be convinced to do so. To motivate strivers, you need to show them how your deal can take them to the next level.

You can build a new relationship with a striver if you have the right tools. Strivers are motivated by access to things they don't have. A striver would love to have dinner with your celebrity friend. Likewise, they would be impressed if you brought them to play golf at an exclusive country club. Take your striver-client to the Super Bowl. Even if the client doesn't love football, they will love the event. Be careful, because strivers are not loyal. Your relationship will only last as long as strivers feel as though you are helping them fill their needs.

This caution is especially important if you put a striver on your team. Remember, they don't really care what their current group thinks of them. The grass is always greener elsewhere for a striver. Strivers join a group (or company) because they believe it offers a situation that is better than their previous one. They will leave if they find a "better" group.

Is it worthwhile to buy the attention of a striver? It certainly can be. But it may be wise to take the striver to the Ryder Cup to celebrate the closing of a big deal instead of as an enticement to a future long-term relationship. Strivers are always looking for the next gig. They do not suffer from an excess of loyalty. Such characteristics are good if you are trying to be the next big gig and not so good if you are trying to keep the striver in your camp.

Negotiating with a Striver . . .

Howard is trying to sell a condo to Harvey. Harvey is a striver, and Howard knows it. Howard repeatedly mentions the former NFL quarterback who lives in the building, as well as the *Sports Illustrated* model who lives in the same complex. If he is really diligent, Howard arranges a meeting or phone call with one of them to endorse the building. Howard may also mention several unnamed "CEOs and big wheels" living there. If you are selling to a Level III striver, find out who he wants to belong with and then figure out a way to make it happen.

Now, assume that Harvey and Howard are negotiating a business deal. Howard is selling widgets to striver Harvey. Harvey likes the product but knows there is competition. What can Howard offer Harvey? It won't hurt to have Harvey meet the ex-pro athlete who is now a manager for Howard's company. But Harvey will need more before he'll make the deal Howard is looking for. Howard invites Harvey to come to town a day early so they can go to the Cubs game the night before the meeting. Joining them for dinner and the game are two of Harvey's friends and the company's ex-jock manager. The friends are fun, and one of them is a minor celebrity. The ex-jock is also fun. Maybe Howard can work out a locker room visit or some post-game elbow rubbing. The evening is designed to give Harvey a good time, and to make him feel part of a special group. This will make it harder for Harvey to walk away the next day when Howard asks for the big order.

Stayers

Stayers are on Level III, but the needs of stayers are much closer to Level II than to Level IV. "Not making waves" is one way to recognize a stayer. Stayers are typically followers operating on Level III.

Body language will help you recognize a stayer. They avoid confrontation, so will often not look you in the eye. If you are proposing a change, stayers tend to sit back, with hands in front of them or arms crossed. This defensive posture reveals that they want to avoid change—they just want things to stay the way they are. Stayers are not risk takers. Often, they will need to talk to someone else before committing to a decision. Stayers don't like risk or drama.

When you recognize a stayer in a business situation, you must confirm whether they are the decision maker. You can waste time and resources with a stayer only to find out they need to check with the boss before doing anything.

If you aren't already doing business with a company, don't put your faith with a stayer. They will be reluctant to change. On the other hand, if you are a long and trusted vendor, seek out stayers because they tend to renew existing relationships.

Negotiating with a Stayer . . .

The difficultly of negotiating with stayers is that they are hard to motivate. Stayers are at Level III and happy to be there. They don't want to move to Level IV so the carrot is ineffective. The best way to motivate a stayer is by fear. The status quo is the only place stayers feel safe. You can get them to act when they are afraid that their apple cart will be upset.

The two futures approach works well with the stayer, but only when you take away the status quo as an option. If you can show them one future that includes the status quo and one that doesn't, they will almost always choose the status quo. This is useful only if the status quo is what you seek. By showing stayers two futures and, at the same time, demonstrating that the status quo is not an option, you can motivate them to agree with you. An example of this follows.

Will is a criminal defense lawyer. Brett is a stayer who works for the District Attorney's Office and has been prosecuting minor cases for twelve years. Brett likes his job, likes plea-bargaining, but doesn't like trial very much. Will knows this.

Will has a client accused of driving under the influence (DUI). No one was hurt and there was no accident. Will is confident that he can win a trial on a technical issue. Will and Brett know that the standard plea bargain in their city for a first-time DUI is thirty days in jail, two years of probation, and a $1,500 fine. Prosecutor Brett, the stayer, is comfortable negotiating in this range, having plea-bargained hundreds of cases over the years. Brett expects to plea bargain this case in the same way.

However, defense lawyer Will knows that Brett is a stayer. For Brett, avoiding the pain of losing a trial or having bad press is more motivating than the glory of winning a trial and putting a defendant away for a long time. So Will employs a two futures close. The status quo would be the standard plea bargain discussed above. Will ignores the status quo and offers to plea-bargain the case, but with no jail time for his client. If Brett insists on jail time, Will promises to take the case to trial. Will has taken the standard plea bargain off the table. Brett's choices now are to agree to the lower sentence or to take the case to trial. Both choices are unpleasant for Brett because he doesn't like to try cases. Will, on the other hand, is happy with either choice: he would like to try the case and he is confident that he can win. At the same time, the plea bargain is a good deal for his client.

That is how to deal with a stayer. The key is to take the status quo off the table, whether you use the two futures close or another approach. If stayers do not have status quo security, they are likely to take the safest route to resolution. Stayers are motivated more by fear than by reward. Remember, they are at Level III, but lean toward Level II (safety). They don't want to get kicked out of the group they belong to. Threats of gravity maneuvers also work well against stayers.

Let's assume Howard is selling a condo to stayer Sam. Howard should emphasize the quiet neighborhood, its tranquil scenery, and the "keep to themselves" neighbors. Sam has no desire to hang out with pro-football players or super models. Whatever would Sam say to a supermodel?

On the other hand, you might find a stayer who is a pro-football player or a supermodel or a CEO. They have earned their way into an exclusive peer group and they want to stay there. Often, these people were strivers and became stayers when they reached their desired peer group. The most obvious examples are newly promoted employees or new country club members.

A good way to get value from stayers is to enhance their sense of belonging. A comment like, "Your boss will be happy about this," or, "This is a big feather in your cap," can work wonders. Some negotiators make it a point, after the deal is closed, to admit to the other side that they (the other side) won the deal. Personally, I don't like to tell the other side that they killed me on the deal unless they actually killed me. Negotiators often think about how a deal will enhance their situation, but can lose sight of this value in the heat of negotiation. Don't hesitate to remind the other side of this value.

When you believe a stayer has to get the deal done, you can create value by temporarily shutting down the negotiation.

Or you can wait a while to respond and create value with less drama. Sometimes this can be as simple as waiting thirty seconds before responding to a question. Often it means responding to an offer in a few days or a week instead of right away.

An ideal way to exploit this situation is to find a number in the favorable side of your range that you believe is also within the other side's acceptable range. Once you determine this number, wait before presenting it. Then present the number as a final number (if it really is) or as a near-final number. By creating anxiety, you create the fear that the stayer will lose this deal and, therefore, exiled from their peer group. But you must understand the risks associated with waiting: don't risk losing the deal unless you are willing to lose it.

Motivation Level IV: Status and Reputation Needs

Level IV players want to be honored members.

Status needs are twofold. First there is reputation: the status and recognition that come from others. Second, there is the self-esteem that comes from within.

Level IV reputation needs are similar to the Level III belonging needs, with one major difference. When people operate at the belonging level (Level III), they need to be recognized as one of the group. When they operate at the reputation level (Level IV), they need to be recognized as a special member of the group. People need to satisfy first their need to belong: "I am one of us." Then some people turn to satisfaction of the reputation-level needs (Level IV): "I am one of us who leads," or, "I am one of us who can finish difficult deals." To demonstrate the difference another way, "I am a member of the club" versus "I am an honored member of the club."

Level IV players often compare themselves to others. Some consider themselves successful based on being recognized as better than others, as opposed to reaching goals for themselves. Ironically, Level IV people are self-centered, but tend to derive their own satisfaction from the opinions of others.

The old saying holds that it's amazing how much can get done if no one cares who gets the credit. People with a Level IV deficit care who gets the credit. They want it. Negotiations can swing based on Level IV negotiators' need to enhance or protect their reputation. Often, a deal will close or not close based on who gets credit for the deal. Be aware of this and be ready to spread credit around to enhance your deal.

Level IV players will often talk about nonbusiness things that matter to them. You can tell a lot about Level IV players by hearing them talk about their kids. Some will brag about their children. Parents who coach often take steps to feature their child. Of course, their child will be the pitcher or quarterback. Some of these parents will push harder to make their child play better. These are all signals that the parent is concerned about their own Level IV needs. A parent living through their musical or athletic child demonstrates their own Level IV deficiency. It is not a coincidence that such parents tend to either be artists or athletes who were highly successful (pro or close to it) or that had no special talent at all. The vast majority of parents (who participated but never came close to the big time) seem less likely to seek fulfillment through their kids' achievements.

Sometimes, the same Level IV-type act has opposing outcomes on a subject's reputation. Consider a politician who presents himself to the community as a hardworking, chaste, family man—but cheats on his wife. If this duplicity is discovered, his reputation will be destroyed. For the family man, loss of reputation in this way can mean loss of marriage, home, family, and maybe his job. (If you recognize all this as a safety concern, you are correct.) On the other hand, consider a rock star who presents himself to the world as a hedonist. If he sleeps with a strange woman on the road, he may do so to fulfill his Level IV need to enhance his reputation as a rock star. Same act, but different impact.

I have come to know many professional athletes after their careers have ended. A pattern evolves in some of these athletes as they watch their kids grow up playing sports. Based on their genetics, most of these kids are good enough to be on the best teams. (Being "on the team"— Level III—is not a concern to the parents.) However, very few of these kids are good enough to enjoy the rare success that their professional athlete parent enjoyed. As the kids grow up, these parents remember the youth sports honors and accolades they enjoyed many years before. Success came to these parents at a young age, so their Level IV needs for reputation and honor were well satisfied early on. In most cases, this reputation was an important self-identifier. So it is natural for parents to become concerned on a Level IV basis when they see that their child may not be enjoying the same type of recognition that came to them at the same age.

Improvers and Impeders

Level IV players come in two types: "improvers" and "impeders." Both types want to be recognized as better than the rest. Improvers work to be better through self-improvement, hard work, and long hours. Impeders work as hard but are more willing to impede the progress of others to achieve their goals. For improvers, a rising tide floats all boats. For impeders, a rising tide helps no one because it raises all boats the same amount.

Level IV players, both improvers and impeders, can be very strong individual performers. To reach Level IV, you must know that you belong in the game. Level IV players ("I want to be a star") will try to control internal systems for their own advantage. They will tend to express strong preferences and will complain if they feel slighted. Level IV players are chasing great things, and expect to accomplish them. They will put in the long hours and diligent work that leads to success. Their success can serve as an example for others. A Level IV player who wants to succeed through hard work can serve as a leader for others and will add to the success of the team by showing others how that success is attained. This is great if the person is an Improver.

Impeders are divisive to team culture. They will be happy if they do well even if the team does not. They would rather hit a home run in a losing game than get no hits in a victory. In a business context, they will not be genuinely happy when a colleague makes a great deal for the company. Impeders tend to be envious of the success of others, which can lead to problems if left unchecked. Improvers, on the other hand, will be happy for their colleague's success and recognition, and will then take steps to improve their own performance so they can be the honored one next time.

An improver can be the best person to lead your group. The improvers want to make themselves and the team better. They are happy when the team succeeds, because improvers understand that if the team does better, their reputation is enhanced. Improvers share credit more readily than impeders.

An impeder can be a negative example. An impeder can be a major distraction and sometimes is not worth the trouble they cause (even as a high achiever). Impeders tend to hog credit and spread blame. At their worst, impeders can bring down a whole team. They can foster negative competition within the group. Imagine a sales team in which members don't support each other, don't share leads, and don't acknowledge each other's accomplishments. This is the impeder culture.

Most high performers first decide that they want to accomplish great things. Often, their motivation is that they want to be a star in the eyes of others. The fundamental difference between improvers and impeders is this: the improver seeks to become a star whereas impeders don't want others to star in their place; improvers want to be recognized as better than others whereas impeders don't want others to be recognized as better than them.

Negotiating with Improvers and Impeders . . .
When dealing with improvers and impeders it is important to remember that these are Level IV actors. The underlying principle is that you will add value to your transaction by improving their status and reputation. Figure out how to do this and you are on your way toward a successful negotiation.

If your counterparts are improvers, show them ways to get better. Sell the improvers on how this deal will enhance their status. Remind them that this is a high-profile deal, in which the press will have regular interest. Remind them that by working with your company, they will be recognized as working with the best organization in the industry. If it is true, show them how their reputation from working on this project will result in additional recognition and new business for them. In the right situation, you can get improvers to give you a better deal in exchange for the long-term benefit to their reputation.

Dealing with impeders is more difficult. You must do all of the same things that you do for an improver and you must add extra finesse. Remember that an impeder is fundamentally seeking recognition but also does not want anyone else to receive recognition. With each and every negotiation with improvers, it is important to remind them of the status the deal will bring to them. When working with impeders, it is also important that you focus the credit and the glory of the transaction on them.

A particular problem arises when you are dealing with two impeders on the same deal. Each will be jealous of the credit and recognition the other gets, regardless of how much they get themselves. Trying to divide the credit between two impeders is an advanced negotiation problem. A way through the problem is to remember that, fundamentally, each one wants the credit. You have to focus on the credit that each one receives and minimize discussion about what the other person will receive. However, misrepresenting the amount of credit the other one will get is the worst possible solution. You need to be honest at all times.

Being honest about the credit each one receives means you work on the emphasis. If the two impeders are Dick and Jane, talk about all of the benefits to Dick when you are with him, and talk about all of the benefits to Jane when you are with her. Each will complain if they think the other is getting undue credit. However, in the end, each is a Level IV actor who wants to make sure they get their own credit. So, with a little finesse, and remembering the type of person you are talking to, you can appropriately divide the credit between two impeders without offending either one.

Another idea is not to deal with impeders. They bring jealousy and drama with them. It is sometimes best to leave them alone. But that is not always possible.

The Pretender: The Curious Intersection of Safety and Status

Some individuals actually operating under Level II (safety) concerns try to mask those concerns by what may appear like Level IV concerns. This is an interesting character called "the pretender." A pretender is experiencing Level II safety concerns, but pretends to be seeking great things. Their safety concerns are typically financial. However, they want to be seen as seeking recognition [Level IV].

> Pretenders are the ones who have a low pair and are trying to bluff their way through the hand.

The pretender combines egotism and insecurity. This person is typically, but not always, male. I have seen the pretender manifest as an aging entrepreneur who approaches retirement or a political leader contemplating leaving office. Typically, this entrepreneur or politician has been successful enough to enjoy good living but has not become wealthy. Often as pretenders contemplate retirement, they may not have the financial means to support a comfortable retirement. This individual has typically lived a life with a concern for appearances. Pretenders belong to a country club, but may not have a college fund for their children. They have an expensive car and, perhaps, a modest home. They may have more debt than savings. While they may not be living beyond their means, they are certainly at the edge of financial insecurity.

At the same time, the pretender has lived life as a leader, typically as a prominent citizen in the community. Pretenders draw energy from people and seek praise from others. They have successfully navigated most of their life by projecting an image that is not supported by their own financial position. They have also lived most of life dealing with safety concerns because they never saved enough money, or gained enough true skill at their job, to feel truly secure. Pretenders don't operate under Level III (belonging) because they are more concerned with being an "honored" member of a group than in joining a different group (an attitude that may have developed over the years because they found they couldn't achieve the status or financial brevity they have, much less that which they desire, elsewhere).

In my work, which often deals with partnership disputes and ownership transitions, I regularly see this personality. It arises sometimes when the aging entrepreneur wants to transition the company to an underling but needs more money to retire than the company can provide. It also arises when a younger partner wants to push out the aging entrepreneur because the entrepreneur is taking a bigger salary (to support his lifestyle) than justified by his current contribution to the company. One recent example demonstrates how to deal with this situation. . . .

A former business partner, Steve, was a significant drag on a thriving business. Though retired, he maintained a 33 percent ownership interest in the company and continued to meddle in the company's management activities. In the five years since his departure, the two remaining partners, Tommy and Randy, had grown the business, had become comfortable operating it, and were poised for further growth. However, Steve's meddling and ownership were millstones around their neck. They approached me seeking a legal way to get rid of Steve.

Steve was a smart and experienced businessman and a good negotiator. He also had serious Level II safety concerns around money. He supported an ex-wife, a current wife, and three adult children. His ego created a need to be the financial patriarch of his family. Putting aside the dysfunction of being the full financial supporter for adult children, it was clear that Steve had Level II financial needs.

One year, the company's auditors informed the partners that they had found an accounting error, which created a significant tax liability for Steve. Tommy, Randy, and I developed a strategy whereby they would use some extra cash they had in the company to purchase Steve's 33 percent share of the company. This would provide him the cash to pay off his tax liability and support his family. It seemed like a terrific opportunity for these two problems to solve each other.

One major problem arose: Steve is a pretender. His status needs would never let him ask for the cash. Pretenders publicly deny their own financial difficulties. Steve would never admit that he needed the cash, even though everybody else knew it was true. Our side agreed that if we approached Steve and directly offered this payment that he would either assume that Tommy and Randy wanted to get rid of him or that he would want to negotiate a better deal than the buyout justified. So, it became critical to the transaction that the buyout plan was Steve's idea. It takes finesse to give someone else an idea. Pulled off with success, it often helps bring a difficult deal to close, and it is the best way to deal with a pretender.

Timing was important to our plan. We started with Tommy and Randy sending Steve the most recent company financials in the normal course of reporting. The company was cash-heavy. While Steve usually pretended not to read the reports, we were fairly certain that he would thoroughly examine these because of his new tax liability. In the same week, the auditors sent notice of the tax liability to all partners. At that point we waited, hoping that Steve would approach us with his own idea of using the excess cash on the company's balance sheet to solve his need for cash. Unfortunately, after two weeks, Steve still had not contacted us.

It became necessary to prod him, so we put together an offer under a provision of the Member Control Agreement that capped the value of his remaining shares under certain cir- cumstances. Using the cap value as a starting point, we sent him a letter offering to buy his shares at a discount. In our letter, we directly tied the tax liability to this offer. Our hope was that this offer would get him to focus on the money and seek to improve our offer. We hoped (and it turned out cor- rectly) that Steve would think it was "his idea" to ask for more money than we offered.

The letter drew a response. A week later we met with all the principals and the lawyers for both sides. At this point, it was also important to understand Steve's motivation. Steve talked about things like legacy and the company that he built and generally gave signals of status (Level IV) and self-ac- tualization (Level V) concerns. However, knowing his per- sonality, and his financial situation (and noticing that each of his negotiating points was actually about money), we were able to correctly discern that Steve's true concerns were about safety (Level II). In short, we had confirmed that Steve needed the money.

A key concern for us was getting a good deal financially—but more important was the terms under which the money changed hands. It was critical for us that Steve be removed from the board and all company offices and that all of his shares be acquired. At the beginning of the meeting the parties were less than $50,000 apart and my clients were willing to go most of the way toward closing that gap to get the terms they wanted. To get these terms, it was important that Steve feel in control of the transaction and that he be permitted to maintain a front (within the room) of not really needing the money. Without significant insight into his motivation, we would not have been able to reach a deal with Steve.

As negotiations proceeded, we employed specific tactics. We always expressed an openness to move on the financial side, but we moved very slowly. We brought up some of our issues around the terms as they arose naturally in the conversation. Like most pretenders, Steve is a talker who prefers to dominate meetings. We used this as an asset by reflecting back to him on points in his own speeches where it helped us to do so. For example, when Steve talked about legacy, we validated that need for him. If he talked for five minutes about past problems and one minute about payment terms, we ignored the problems and focused on the terms.

We entered the meeting hoping to close the deal and made this intention clear to the other side prior to the meeting. Then, at the appropriate time during the meeting, we caucused separately. We came back from the caucus with a series of conditions, all of which we had decided on before the meeting but had nevertheless come up during the course of Steve's discussions. They were "his ideas." Some conditions were concessions to Steve's side. For instance, we agreed to take him off of a company loan guaranty.

After the caucus, we put all of the conditions on the table and asked the other side for a new number. It was their turn to provide a number, which worked to our advantage. When they put their number on the table, we again asked for another short caucus. We came back this time with a new number that we knew would close the deal financially and we attached it to all of the conditions that we had placed on the table before. As we had hoped, Steve's own actions were dominated by his Level II safety concerns—he wanted the money. He accepted our offer.

> The pretender's insecurity and arrogance often have the same voice but rarely have the same words. True Level IV players seek something other than financial gain.

The key to closing this transaction was understanding the pretender. Insecurity and arrogance often have the same voice but rarely have the same words. Pretenders exhibit the signs of Level II concerns, acting like they have safety concerns. They often reveal anxiety to get a deal done. They reference finances. True Level IV actors typically seek something other than financial gain. They often work to get the deal done but want to make sure they receive the credit or that they get to do the important work. A pretender will not pick up the check at lunch, while a Level IV actor is quick to do so. The pretender wants to save the money, and the Level IV actor wants to be the leader. In the scenario with Steve, it was very helpful that we actually understood Steve's financial situation. With this information we were secure in knowing that he needed the money and that this Level II safety need was driving his decision making.

In the end, knowing that Steve was a pretender enabled us to devise a plan to get the results we wanted.

Motivation Level V: Growth and Self-Actualization Needs

What is Self Actualization? Self-actualization, broadly speaking, means growth. It is the ability to reach one's full potential. According to Maslow, common traits among people who are self-actualized are:

- Embracing reality and facts rather than denying truth
- Acting spontaneously
- Focusing on problems outside of themselves
- Accepting their own human nature with all of its shortcomings in stoic style, and projecting a similar acceptance of the same in others

These definitions are all very well in the world of psychology but they do not work as well in the world of negotiation. For negotiation purposes, the best definition of "self-actualization" is *a desire for growth*. People acting on Level V or striving for Level V want to expand beyond their current situation. A Level V actor might be a PhD. who wants to become a physician, or a physician who wants to get a PhD. In business, there are very few self-actualized middle managers. If a middle manager wants to expand or grow by virtue of a promotion, they are probably working on Level III as a striver, or Level IV as one seeking status. If a middle manager seeks self-actualization, it usually is manifested not within a desire to grow a corporation, but rather outside of it. A middle manager whose goal is to coach his twelve-year-old to a state hockey championship is seeking self-actualization through the hockey coaching. A middle manager whose primary avocation is yoga might be seeking self-actualization through that. However, it is important not to confuse the desire for a promotion with a desire for growth into self-actualization.

Someone seeking self-actualization will usually be heavily engaged in something that, to the outsider, has no apparent reward. An amateur musician or painter, whose work will never be sold to or appreciated by the masses, could be seeking self-actualization. The work does not even need to be great. It just needs to be fulfilling to the individual.

Though many strive for it, few people reach Level V. If you find yourself dealing with someone who appears to have satisfied their Level IV needs, you should consider how to bring them closer to self-actualization. You can command great value if you provide self-actualization.

One example of trying to satisfy self-actualization needs is the huge sums that sports team owners pay to their athletes. Often, winning a World Series or a Super Bowl represents self-actualization to the team owner. A mega-successful businessman might well find himself fully satisfied on the first four levels of Maslow's needs. However, he may also find that he is not self-actualized. Thus, a businessman who has everything material continues to look for the next challenge. In some cases, self-actualization is manifest through fights for justice (Martin Luther King, Jr.). In other cases, it is an effort to become the very best at one's profession (Tiger Woods). In still others, it is a desire to be known as a celebrity (Donald Trump).

The signs of someone seeking self-actualization are sublevels of Level V. If you see signs that someone is either seeking to know, understand, and explore, or is preoccupied with the order or beauty of a situation, they might be acting at Level V.

One of the signs of interest in self-actualization is dissatisfaction with what appears to be a successful career. Another is the diminishment of interest in things like business and contract negotiations. If you are dealing with someone who has reached the top of their profession and is talking about social issues (or gardening or sailing or another hobby) at a time when they really ought to be thinking about business, you can help them. If you nurture their desire for self-actualization, you accomplish two things. First, they will like you.

Second, they will grow more interested in becoming self-actualized and less interested in the contractual details. Both of these are likely to help you create more value for your side of the deal.

Here is an example: Hal and Sally are negotiating on opposite sides of a union contract renewal. During the negotiations, Hal notices that Sally has returned to a questioning mode at a time when they should be moving toward close. Sally's questions are not really about controversial contract provisions, but are directed more generally toward business operations and the future impact of certain provisions they have already agreed upon. Hal is worried until he realizes that Sally is not trying to reopen these provisions, but just wants to learn more about the industry and operations for her own education. By understanding that Sally is working at the Level V sublevel of "seeking cognitive knowledge," Hal is able to respond and then put the deal on track for closing.

If you see someone showing signs of seeking self-actualization, you should consider ways to provide it. For example, if you run into CEO Bob who talks about wanting to teach high school math, you will get more value out of a deal by showing him how this transaction will help him reach that goal. You might even get him to do some free training for you.

Self-Actualization is Expensive

One of my favorite movie negotiating scenes occurs toward the end of *Jerry McGuire* (1996). Jerry is a football agent whose client just became a hero on national television by catching the winning touchdown pass. The game is over, the home team has won, and everyone is celebrating. Jerry is standing outside the locker room as the crowd embraces the team's jubilant owner. Jerry catches the owner's eye and gives him the "money" signal, rubbing his thumb and fingers together. The smiling owner says, "I know, I know." Jerry has effectively moved the negotiations to a higher level, which will result in riches for his client. The owner, a sophisticated nego-tiator, knows his player's value has just risen dramatically and is willing to pay for it. Why? Because the player's victorious catch helped the owner achieve self-actualization.

SKILL #6
Research

Knowledge of the opposition is critical. You need to find out as much as you can about your opponent and your transaction. The information you gather will be restricted by, but within, your time and expense budgets.

Know Your Industry

You need to understand your industry. If you are a lawyer or other hired negotiator, you need to understand the industry of your client. Understanding your industry means knowing its history, knowing its leaders (personally, if possible), and knowing how it is affected by macro and micro trends.

You need to constantly update your research skills. If your business can afford it, you should have dedicated staff that spends most of their time on research.

Know the Person On the Other Side of the Negotiation Table

It is a good idea to research people on the other side of a transaction. In one case, I was litigating on behalf of a client. We believed that our client was owed $75,000 under a contract. The other side acknowledged the debt, but claimed that business had been so bad (they were in an industry that suffered during the recession) that they simply did not have the money to pay it. Doing a simple search on Google, I found out some obvious things. The company had moved from a more expensive office to a less expensive office. However, I also discovered that the principal and his wife had moved to a bigger house in a prestigious suburb. The couple belonged to a country club, and the socialite wife appeared at charity balls frequented by the country club set.

The couple was spending a great deal of money on their house, their country club membership, and black-tie charity events. This money was serving to enhance their reputation. In short, they were trying to appear as if they were a wealthy young couple. I was able to conclude from this that they had at least some money to spend and that they could be motivated by a threat to their reputation.

I was also able to do additional research through contacts close to the couple. You can find contacts close to your opposition through sites like Facebook and Linked-In. After a few conversations, I knew the business was not doing very well, and also concluded that the husband probably had not told his wife this information. She had purchased a new BMW less than six months earlier. Armed with this information, we set up separate depositions of the business owner and his wife for a date thirty days ahead. Ultimately, we were able to work out a favorable settlement.

There is special software available, for a price, to do background research on individuals. However, most people do not need to do this. There is a great deal of information now available on the Internet. With simple searches you can determine, for example, that a lawyer has not updated his biography in seven years. This might mean that he is too busy to update his biography. Or, it might mean that he doesn't pay attention to details. Test him and find out.

There are many inexpensive resources to help you find out information about businesses. You should always look up the company's website. By examining the company's website, you can get a glimpse into the way they do business and the image they want to portray. You may also gain insight into the people you are negotiating with. If, for example, the website features the CEO/entrepreneur in a photo on the front page, that will tell you something about that entrepreneur's self-image. If the website it outdated, that is useful information. Services like ZoomInfo.com as well as the Dun & Bradstreet can help you find company information. Bloomberg.com provides succinct company profiles of publicly-held companies and allows you to access 10-Q and other SEC filings of a particular company. In Minnesota, nonprofit companies are required to file annual reports with the state. These reports contain only broad financial information, but they can be very helpful.

This was the case in a negotiation between a physician's clinic against an HMO. From the public filings, I was able to discern that the spread between the premiums collected by the HMO and the actual claims paid by the HMO had increased each of the previous five years. The average annual increase was more than 20 percent; thus, the HMO's "gross profit" (premiums collected minus claims paid) had more than doubled in five years.

At the meeting, the HMO took the position we expected them to take. They claimed that everyone had a duty to hold healthcare costs down, including the doctors. The doctors are well paid and need to accept only minor increases because of the additional cost of healthcare administration. The negotiator was surprised when I called him out on this point. I reminded him that his HMO had increased its annual take by more than 100 percent in the same period that our reimbursements had increased by less than 10 percent. The negotiator was genuinely surprised and denied that it was true. However, when I showed him the report (which I had with me) he abandoned the "healthcare cost" argument completely.

In addition to winning that particular argument, the exchange also gave me significant credibility with the other side. That piece of research played a key role in my team obtaining a good result for our client.

In research, remember to use any contacts that you might have. Think of people who know the other side and who also know you. Do you know anyone who works at the company? Do you know anyone who went to school where your counterpart went to school? This type of inside information can be very useful. The more you know about a person and their background, the better chance you have to motivate them to do what you want them to do.

In addition, it is important to do research on the transaction itself. What are you buying? What are the weaknesses you can exploit? Are there better products for your use? How many factories are in China that could actually manufacture your product? What is your competition doing? What is their competition doing? Find out everything you can that affects the transaction, and you will find something that will help you in your negotiation.

There is also basic information-gathering work you should be doing every day within your industry. Read the trade publications that pertain to your industry. The cumulative positive affect of reading these publications over a long period of time is that you earn a reputation as an expert in your industry, specifically in current events in your industry. If you spend time in a particular industry, you should keep up with the leading trade publications. Trades establish the conventional wisdom within the industry. This is a fulcrum by which you can leverage your opponents.

Imagine you are in the widget industry. The trades for a particular month all talk about a piece of legislation that will have a significant, but not obvious, impact on the widget industry. If your opponent is not aware of this legislation, you can be certain that he does not read the trades. If he is aware of the issue, you can have a conversation with him that will help you assess him in other ways.

To the extent your customers are focused in a particular industry, you should read their trade publications as well. As a lawyer for many radio stations, I try to become an expert in industry events. By reviewing the right trade publications, you can occasionally provide insight to your client that they will appreciate getting. Sometimes this is just gossip ("I saw that Smith left ABC Corp.") but sometimes it is true business insight that will help your client's company perform better. From a negotiation perspective, understanding the industry makes you an expert at the negotiation table. This gives you control of the situation.

Research is critical to preparation for any negotiation. By efficiently conducting research, you know more going into negotiation than your opponent does. This allows you to drive the transaction where you want to drive it.

SKILL #7
Communication Skills

> Understanding is the key to communication.
> Communication is the key to motivation.

Strong communication skills are critical to being a successful negotiator. Regardless of how highly skilled and well prepared you are, if you are not a strong communicator, you won't maximize your deal opportunities. Good communication skills require the ability to listen, the ability to think clearly, and to communicate persuasively in writing, by telephone, and in person. The primary (and most neglected) negotiation skill is listening.

Listening
Listening skills are very important, as discussed above. I want to mention listening here only to remind you that no communication skill is more important than listening. Read chapter 2 (Interviewing and Listening), and be sure to understand the discussion there. You must be a good listener to be a strong communicator. Listen. Listen. Listen.

Speaking

To clearly express your thoughts verbally, you must first think clearly. Clear thinking means focusing on the heart of the matter without distraction. Clear thinking is the product of full understanding and full preparation. To reach this level of focus, you must remove distractions by undertaking complete preparation.

A friend of mine races sailboats. He talks about clear thinking in terms of sailing. In sailing, the bow of the boat must be kept absolutely clean because any little debris interferes with the speed of the boat. If a piece of seaweed gets caught on the front of the boat, it will destroy the perfectly aerodynamic design of the hull. You must get rid of the seaweed.

Clear thinking is achieved by discarding or ignoring all of the ancillary matters and focusing on what is really important. A fair question arises: How do you get rid of the seaweed? To repeat, clear thinking is the product of full understanding and full preparation.

You think clearly by preparing fully. Full preparation gives us the ability to understand which deal points and arguments matter and which are simply dead ends. Chapter 3 of this book is all about preparation. Read it again, if you need to.

Clear understanding is related to full preparation but is not the same thing. Clear understanding is broader. It's what you know from your experience and your personal development. Full preparation means you are ready for this transaction. Full understanding means you are ready for any transaction in this area.

Every first-year law student in the country takes a civil procedure class. The well-thought-out and intricate rules of civil procedure govern litigation. When I was in law school, I memorized the important rules but I certainly did not understand them. After a year of working with the rules in litigation, as a practicing lawyer, I was able to see connections between the rules and understand why particular rules, which seemed counterintuitive, were written as they are. After about three years and thousands of hours of litigation, I truly understood the rules of civil procedure. This understanding enabled me to litigate far more effectively, because I knew why there were wrinkles that represented either dead ends or opportunity for advancement.

After twenty years, I still read the *Rules of Civil Procedure* from front to back once a year. This important practice keeps me sharp. However, the rules are so engrained in me at this point in time that I have to force myself to slow down when I read them. This is what true understanding is.

By gaining full understanding and undertaking full preparation, you can begin to think clearly about the matter at hand. Only when you think clearly can you communicate clearly.

A good example of not thinking clearly happened a few years ago when I rented a car and was driving through upstate New York. I was going over the speed limit when I heard the police sirens behind me. I pulled over but I could not find the button to get the window down. I didn't fully understand how to operate the rental car; I had not fully prepared by mapping out all of the buttons before I started driving. As the police officer stood outside of the car, peering through the closed window, demanding that I lower it, I repeatedly pressed the button to make the doors lock and unlock. I was not thinking clearly and the situation grew worse as the stress increased. Finally, I opened the door and stepped out of the car. This definitely raised the intensity of the situation and did not make the policeman happy. With my hands in the air I explained that I didn't know how to open the windows of the rental car. The police officer understood and was kind enough to let me go with a warning, after I demonstrated that I hadn't been drinking and after he showed me where the window button was located. I wasn't prepared for the situation and, had it been a negotiation, I would have lost.

Once you can think clearly, you can develop the strategies and tactics necessary to maximize your opportunity in a negotiation. To revisit the example above, assume that I was driving my own car when the police pulled me over. I know where the buttons are. I would have immediately prepared for the conversation by rolling the window down, and taking out my license and insurance card. I would have employed the strategy I always do in such situations, which is to be polite, do what the officer says, and hope for the best. Perhaps I still would have been given a ticket, but the situation certainly would have been less stressful.

Once you have fully analyzed a situation, you can think about how to clearly and persuasively express your thoughts. Understanding is the key to communication. Communication is the key to persuasion.

The Four Rules of Communication

1. Understand the strengths and weaknesses of each communication medium.
2. Know your audience.
3. Less is More.
4. Listen. Listen. Listen.

The Four Rules of Communication

In today's world, you can communicate by sending an email, by talking on the phone, or by meeting your counterpart in person. I still, occasionally, send letters by U.S. mail, but rarely. This book is not the right forum to teach you everything about how to communicate clearly, but there is room to share the primary rules with you. If you understand the four primary rules, you can quickly improve your communication skills. People spend their whole lives improving their ability to communicate. You can't begin this soon enough.

Rule 1: Understand the strengths and weaknesses of each communication medium.

You need to understand the advantages and disadvantages of each form of communication and decide in each instance which method is the best to use. Meeting with someone in person is the most efficient and spontaneous way to communicate, once the meeting begins. It is the most personal way to communicate. A telephone call is still personal and spontaneous, but it is somewhat more difficult to convey complex ideas. Video conferences are seeing broader use and are really a combination of the telephone and in-person meetings. They carry the added value of visual communication without the expense of travel.

Email is the least expensive and easiest way to communicate. It is also one of the least effective means of serious communication. Because you cannot change your tone of voice or display nuance, emails are at times misunderstood. However, with email, you have the ability to state exactly what you want to state, have a written record of it, and communicate it immediately to your counterpart. An artfully drafted email can appear to have been written spontaneously when, in fact, it was meticulously prepared.

Rule 2: Know your audience.

You must know your audience. Listeners easily understand strong communication. When I am arguing before a judge, I explain the law differently than if I am explaining the same law to a group of lawyers at an educational seminar or to friends at a cocktail party. Typically, the judge is more interested in a concise explanation than in being entertained. In the educational context, the students want to understand nuance and various applications of the law. In an educational seminar, I often explore dead ends and explain why they are dead ends. As mentioned earlier, I completely ignore extraneous applications of the law when I am arguing before a judge. At a cocktail party, the best things to do are over-simplify the law, add a punch line, and then ask your spectators about their kids.

Rule 3: Less is more.

Know when to stop. Do not bury your point. You need to stop talking (or writing) after you have made your point. If someone asks you for the time of day, just say, "Four o'clock." Don't say, "It is four p.m. and I know this because five minutes ago I looked at my watch and it was three fifty-five . . ."

Too many people talk too long. Use fewer and simpler words when possible. In most instances, when somebody asks you about the weather outside, they want to know if it is hot, cold, sunny, or rainy. They don't need to know the barometric pressure. They don't need to know that the cumulonimbus clouds are forming or that there is a front coming in from the west. They just need to know whether they should wear a sweater or bring their umbrella.

Rule 4: Listen, Listen, Listen.

In case we have not addressed this subject enough, you need to be an active listener. Work on this skill continually.

SKILL #8
Endgame and Closing

Endgame negotiation skills are important for two reasons. The more important reason is the ability to close the deal. Almost as important is the ability to bring more pieces to your side at the end of your deal. Sales people know that a 5 percent margin on $100,000 is more than a 20 percent margin on nothing. (This is not to say that it is always good to complete a deal at any cost. That is not true.) The point is that if you want to close a deal, you need the skills to do so. Here are some important closing techniques.

Seasoning

The first rule of closing is not to try to close prematurely. You must wait until your counterpart is ready to close. Your counterpart will not close until their motivation level is satisfied or threatened to the point where they want to complete the deal. This process is called "seasoning." Expert closers know when their counterpart is ready for closing and how to get there as efficiently as possible.

The term *seasoning* really means, "the maturing of your opponent's needs." But it is more than that. It is a process by which the negotiator eventually becomes ready to make a decision. It is a combination of a passage of time, consideration of various options, and evolving discussions that eventually create, in the negotiator, the motivation to reach an agreement.

Broadly speaking, seasoning can be discussed in three steps. The first step is shopping, the second step is testing, and the third step is closing. In the shopping stage, the negotiator is doing two things. He is determining what his options are and qualifying those options. At the consumer level, the shopping stage includes going to various stores to find, for example, a red compact car that gets at least thirty miles per gallon but costs less than $25,000. In our example, the buyer shops online and goes to various dealerships and determines that there are five different models that satisfy these qualifications. On our shopper's first visit to the dealer, the salesman should not try to close the transaction. Our shopper is not ready to buy, not properly seasoned! Of the five models that qualify, let's assume three of them are better than the other two and it is one of those three that our shopper will buy. This leads our shopper to the second stage, which is negotiation.

In the testing stage the buyer is examining the cars to determine which the best deal. The buyer does this by talking to each dealer and comparing prices and features, examining the history of the vehicles, discovering desirable features of each one, etc. The buyer is further narrowing the choices.

At this point, it is possible, but unlikely, that a salesman would succeed in bringing this shopper directly to closing. The shopper must eliminate the unqualified models while exploring the best deal. Sometimes someone on the opposite side will, at this stage, offer a tremendous deal that is too good to pass up, and the shopper will close. In a typical negotiation, however, more is given away than would have been if you had just waited a little bit longer.

In the third stage, closing, our shopper has decided to buy a car. The shopper has probably narrowed the choice down to two models, knowing the winner will be whichever ends up being the best deal. They no longer consider the third option, as it has been eliminated through the earlier testing and discovery process. Now, the buyer is trying to pit the remaining two models against each other. This shopper is fully seasoned and ready to buy.

The seasoning process is subtler in the business process but the steps are the same. Use very direct, strategic questions to determine the stage your opponents are in. Ask them what (or who) else they are considering. One great closing question is, "If I can get to X price, are you ready to buy today?" This strategy creates certainty for you in understanding how seasoned a person is.

Here is an example of how it works. Assume the landlord is trying to entice the potential tenant to switch to the landlord's building. This is the first meeting. The tenant is viewing the space for the first time.

Landlord: What did you think of the space?

Tenant: I like the location. It is just the size we are looking for. It really is a nice space.

Landlord: What other spaces are you looking at?

Tenant: We are looking at two other buildings today and two others tomorrow. We're definitely interested.

Landlord (closing too soon): We can bring our rate down to fifteen dollars per foot if you can sign up this week.

Tenant: Well, we're interested but we're not ready to decide on which space we want yet.

The landlord made his $15-per-foot offer while the tenant was obviously still shopping. The tenant made it clear that he had other places to look. By throwing out a new number, the landlord set the cap for his space and will very likely have to negotiate a lower rate if he's going to rent that space. Fast forward to the time when the tenant is actually fully seasoned and working on closing. The contest is now between the landlord and the second landlord. Knowing that he can get the first space for $15 per foot, the tenant has this discussion with the second landlord:

> Tenant: The other landlord offered me that space at fifteen dollars per foot right out of the box. I know he will come down from there. What can you do on the rate?

> Second Landlord: Well, I know his location is a little better than mine but I would really like to have you here. I can take it to fourteen dollars per foot but I can't do any better than that.

Now the tenant goes back to the original landlord and has this discussion:

> Tenant: Listen, this is between you and the other landlord's building but he is doing much better on price. He is at thirteen dollars per foot; if you can match him, I will sign up with you. If you can't, then I am going to go with him.

> Landlord: Okay, we can do thirteen dollars per foot.

The deal is signed. However, the landlord prematurely closing on an unseasoned applicant probably cost himself money on the lease rate. By blurting out $15 per foot when he was listed at $18 per foot, he enabled the tenant to get a lower bid from a lesser building. The landlord then had to match that lower price in order to get the tenant. This is the risk of closing on an unseasoned counterpart.

Here's another example to consider. When an employer seeks to hire a new employee, they know the unemployed person is motivated by the opportunity to get a job. That person is ready to take the job and start as soon as possible. Therefore, it takes very little seasoning of the job applicant before the employer can successfully make a job offer.

On the other hand, an employer who is trying to lure a superstar away from a competitor has to think about seasoning. The employer knows that this person can help the company. However, the employer also knows that to move too quickly will result in this person not being as anxious to take the job. A sort of courtship ensues where the two parties get to know each other a little bit and, at some point, they decide whether they are going to work together. In this method, the new employer acted less interested in the potential employee to increased interest in the potential employee.

This brings up an interesting point on seasoning. You don't have to do all of the seasoning yourself. In the first situation above, the job applicant has been seasoned by the job search, by looking for work and being rejected. This fully seasons the job applicant. Suddenly working is better than not working. This takes very little time. The lateral hire, on the other hand, already has a job. This person has to be motivated both to leave the current job and take the job you are offering. This can take weeks or months of discussions.

In business-to-business negotiation, sellers know that it is much easier to sell if the buyers have already expressed an interest in buying. Such a buyer has been seasoned by external events or circumstances. A buyer who cold calls prospects without knowing whether they are ready to buy has to endure the entire seasoning process.

Parties can be seasoned by your actions or by external events. Often, a buyer needs to shop their needs around to determine that you are the best one to buy from. In a new relationship, this seasoning includes a period of building trust. Anything that can change motivation, either instantly or gradually, will potentially season your counterpart and bring you closer to making a deal.

Fundamentals of Closing

Closing an agreement is like scoring a touchdown in a football game—it is an easy thing to do if everything else is properly in place. The difficult part is to make sure that everything is properly in place.

You should start thinking about closing from the very beginning. You should start acting toward closing when you have reached your goal in the negotiations and your counterpart is properly seasoned.

Once your goal is in sight, then you can begin to think about whether it is the time to close. You have to look at several things: consider whether your opponent is fully seasoned, consider the best method for closing, and then create your endgame strategy. Your opponent is ready to close when they are ready to make the decision that you want them to make. By understanding your opponent's motivation, you understand what it will take to make them get to this decision. There are several fundamental closing tactics.

Silence

Silence is an underused closing tactic. Silence is a companion of patience. Patience is an acquired skill. The film *Glengarry Glen Ross* (1992) has an amazing scene in which Jack Lemmon describes closing with silence. According to Lemmon, he sat at the target's kitchen table for eighteen minutes in total silence until his target finally picked up the pen and signed the real estate purchase agreement.

Silence can mean sitting in a meeting and being quiet for long periods of time. It can mean making a slight hesitation before jumping in with your next position. Or, it can mean waiting several days to respond to an offer, instead of responding immediately.

Silence is an asset. It is nearly impossible to close a deal unless your opponent either has everything needed, or believes that everything you are able to give has been given. A period of silence reminds your opponent that your acceptance of an offer (or your response to the opposing position) is not easy for you to do. It has taken thought and consideration and is probably a close call. This means that you might walk away from the deal. This can create the fear that you actually will walk away. This can all be said by saying nothing.

As discussed above, the other side will be fully seasoned when they feel they have earned their position. Silence, hesitation, and slow responses can help make the point to the other side that they have earned their position and you are willing to close the deal.

Split-the-Difference Close

The split-the-difference close is used when two parties are close but can't quite come together. One party offers to "split the difference" in an effort to close the deal. Sometimes this works. I don't like this closing method because the other party can gain an advantage by simply rejecting your overture. Now you have conceded to a new number and they haven't. Artful negotiators can use this concession to bring you closer to their side than your own.

Imagine Ted wants to sell his business for $3.8 million. Ed is willing to buy the business but will only pay $3.7 million. The parties are only $100,000 apart. Ed offers to split the difference, which indicates that he is willing to pay $3.75 million for the business. Ted's next move is simply to decline. The endgame plays out something like this.

Ted [declining the split-the-difference close]: I've told you that I really can't accept less than $3.8 million. I appreciate that you are willing to pay $3.75 million. But if that is your best number, I don't think we can do a deal.

Ed: Well, I am only willing to pay $3.75 million if it will get the deal done. My highest number is $3.7 million.

Ted: Yeah, but it seems a shame to let the deal go over $50,000. You will make that much in revenue in the first month. However, I understand we each have our own estimate of what the business is worth. I believe it is worth

$3.8 million; and if I can't sell it to you for that price, I will just sell it to the next guy.

Now Ed is in a hard place. Ted knows he's willing to pay $3.75 million. Ted thinks he is probably willing to pay $3.8 million. However, Ted is about to walk away from the deal. After some more conversation in which Ed tests Ted's resolve to stay at $3.8 million, the following conversation ensues.

Ted: I have to have $3.8 million, but I will tell you what I can do. I will take $3.75 million now and you can pay me $50,000 after twelve months. That should give you plenty of time to put aside those reserves.

Ed: Okay, we have a deal.

If you decide to use the split-the-difference close, you have to be absolutely clear that splitting the difference is not only your last number but it is beyond your last number (if this is true). You must be willing to walk away if the other side will not split the difference. I don't mean you have to pretend to be willing to walk away—you have to actually be willing to walk away from the deal if they do not agree to split the difference.

False Withdrawal: The Doorknob Close

The doorknob close is a false withdrawal from negotiations. I learned this closing technique from my father, a broadcaster who began his career as a radio salesperson. The doorknob close is useful in many different situations.

It gets its name from the following scenario: The parties are sitting at the conference room table negotiating a deal. The negotiations grind to a halt. Our side knows that the other side has one more chip left to play. We also know that the counterpart is not quite ready to close. The other side is concerned that if they give up their last chip, it will be rejected and the sale will be lost. So they politely get up and begin to walk out of the room. But when their hand touches the doorknob, they stop, turn back, and say, "Wait a minute, what if . . . " and then put the last chip on the table. This is a masterful close because buyer's remorse will often combine with the last chip to close the deal.

The doorknob close is not restricted to its literal meaning. My favorite doorknob close story comes from an attorney friend. My friend was the lead on the settlement negotiation team in a huge class action lawsuit. Billions of dollars were at stake, so as the trial continued through several weeks, the negotiating teams met daily. My friend's firm was local and the opposing team was from out of town. At the end, the opposition used the doorknob close no less than three times in forty-eight hours. As negotiations broke down, the visiting team would declare an impasse, pack up, and head to the airport. Then they would call from the airport with "a new idea to discuss" and the negotiations would continue. In the end, the case settled before the jury came back. My friend went home and burned the clothes she had worn throughout the last seventy-two hours of negotiations.

Two Futures Close

Closing is about getting the other side to make the decision you want them to make. You can often motivate the other side to do this by showing them that failure to decide has consequences. The two futures close is a variety of the hybrid approach (and both were discussed previously, within the motivation section of chapter 5). In the two futures close, you show your opponent two options and you explain the consequences of each.

Assume you are a litigation defense attorney. A plaintiff has made a claim against your client. As negotiations have progressed, you have offered $65,000. You aren't willing to pay more than $75,000 to settle the case. As a last attempt to close before the litigation commences, you point out that you have increased your offer to $75,000 and this will be your final offer. You point out to the plaintiff that his choice is to either accept the $75,000 check today with all of the good things—spell those out—that go with that. Or, he can spend the next year immersed in litigation and spend $50,000 on his own lawyer. Framed properly, your preferred alternative can appear to be very attractive.

These are just a few of the many ways to close a deal. If you combine these tactics with a thorough knowledge of your counterpart's motivation, closing comes naturally and often.

Conclusion

So we return to the parable of Bill and Frank. Re-read the example for skill 5. What did Bill do right? What could he have done differently? How about Frank?

Negotiation is personal. This principle applies to you as well. By reading this book, you have taken your first step toward becoming a BIG FORCE negotiator. You now understand the basic principles of negotiation and the skills that you will need to master them. This is just the beginning. To become a master negotiator, you need to constantly upgrade and refine your facilities in these areas. Improvement comes from constant and steady work. Do the work.

In the immortal words of Voltaire: "We must cultivate our garden." With this book, you have planted the seeds in your BIG FORCE negotiator garden. Now you must cultivate it. Keep working and giving your negotiation skills regular attention and your garden will grow.

About the Author

Terry Moore is an attorney in Minneapolis, Minnesota. He has been practicing the art of negotiation as a business lawyer, litigator and consumer since 1988. His clients include baseball teams, radio and television networks and stations, medical clinics and other businesses of many different types and sizes.

This is Terry's first book. He has written many articles and is a frequent lecturer. Recent subjects include negotiation of sports broadcast rights agreements, litigation and "The Seven Deadly Sins of Mediation".

Terry lives in Edina, Minnesota with his wife, Dr. Anne Moore and their three children, Maddy, T.J. and Auggie.